LOS ANGELES BY NIGHT

Frommer's

LOS ANGELES
by Night

BY

JEFF SPURRIER

A BALLIETT & FITZGERALD BOOK

MACMILLAN • USA

a disclaimer

Prices fluctuate in the course of time, and travel information changes under the impact of the varied and volatile factors that influence the travel industry. Neither the author nor the publisher can be held responsible for the experiences of readers while traveling. Readers are invited to write to the publisher with ideas, comments, and suggestions for future editions.

about the author

Jeff Spurrier writes regularly for *Details,* the *Los Angeles Times, Outside,* and Japanese magazines, and believes that like Norma Desmond, Los Angeles looks better under low light.

Balliett & Fitzgerald, Inc.
Executive editor: Tom Dyja
Managing editor: Duncan Bock
Associate editor: Howard Slatkin
Assistant editor: Maria Fernandez
Editorial assistant: Brooke Holmes

Macmillan Travel art director: Michele Laseau

All maps © Simon & Schuster, Inc.

MACMILLAN TRAVEL
A Simon & Schuster Macmillan Company
1633 Broadway
New York, NY 10019

ISBN 0-02-861127-6
ISSN TK 1088-4718

special sales

Bulk purchases (10+ copies) of Frommer's Travel Guides are available to corporations at special discounts. The Special Sales Department can produce custom editions to be used as premiums and/or for sales promotions to suit individual needs. Existing editions can be produced with custom cover imprints such as corporate logos. For more information write to: Special Sales, Simon & Schuster, 1633 Broadway, New York, NY 10019.

Manufactured in the United States of America

contents

Los Angeles Orientation

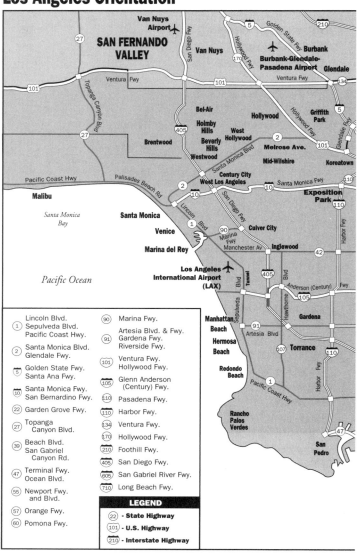

Lincoln Blvd.
(1) Sepulveda Blvd.
Pacific Coast Hwy.

(2) Santa Monica Blvd.
Glendale Fwy.

(5) Golden State Fwy.
Santa Ana Fwy.

(10) Santa Monica Fwy.
San Bernardino Fwy.

(22) Garden Grove Fwy.

(27) Topanga
Canyon Blvd.

(39) Beach Blvd.
San Gabriel
Canyon Rd.

(47) Terminal Fwy.
Ocean Blvd.

(55) Newport Fwy.
and Blvd.

(57) Orange Fwy.

(60) Pomona Fwy.

(90) Marina Fwy.

(91) Artesia Blvd. & Fwy.
Gardena Fwy.
Riverside Fwy.

(101) Ventura Fwy.
Hollywood Fwy.

(105) Glenn Anderson
(Century) Fwy.

(110) Pasadena Fwy.

(110) Harbor Fwy.

(134) Ventura Fwy.

(170) Hollywood Fwy.

(210) Foothill Fwy.

(405) San Diego Fwy.

(605) San Gabriel River Fwy.

(710) Long Beach Fwy.

LEGEND

(22) - State Highway

(101) - U.S. Highway

(210) - Interstate Highway

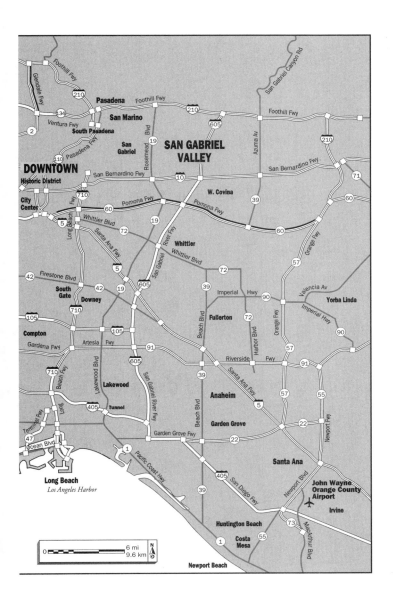

what's
hot,
what's
not

To the uninitiated, Los Angeles may look as flat and anonymous as its unrelenting stream of strip malls and low, square-topped buildings. Don't be fooled. No matter how specific your entertainment demands are, this city has got what you want.

When you head out into the L.A. night, remember that nothing is sacred (except maybe the status of the car you are piloting). Begin with a map, a sense of purpose, and absolutely no expectations. Are you simply dying to see *Beauty and the Beast* at the **Shubert**? How about spilling a glass of wine on the leather coat of Chili Pepper Anthony Kiedis at **Jones**? He's gracious, friendly. Just back from Europe and willing to chat. If you want to pay tribute to Faulkner and L.A. in the thirties, try to break your screenwriter's block with a whiskey soda at **Musso & Frank's** landmark watering hole. At scene maker Brent Bolthouse's *très* happening **Opium Den**, the tide is running high, with wall-to-wall club kids lining up for the next dry martini. Or you could go cruising on Santa Monica Boulevard in West Hollywood (known affectionately in the gay community as WeHo), dropping by **Mani's Bakery** for a coffee, then out to the strip again, hoping to finally meet that guy or gal of your dreams... the one who will make great crepes the next morning. What do you want? It's up to you. Just make sure you remember the car.

What's hot

The caffeine scene... Somewhere on the time line between the go-go eighties and the reemergence of recreational heroin use, L.A. discovered pleasure in a sober alternative to crass materialism and tequila hangovers. Welcome to the Beat Generation, Part II. Like every emergent late-night species, it needed a safe habitat. The L.A. coffeehouse scene developed its own style, complete with stars (your basic folkie–poet–performance artist–comic–raconteur), extras (pierced and tattooed espresso jerks), costumes (pre-Gap grunge wear), and decor (mismatched thrift-store couches, sofas, easy chairs). Go see the real thing, not Starbucks (See The Bar Scene).

Lounge culture... L.A.'s finest contribution to the nineties: a twist more refined than grunge, a spritz more ironic than Armani, and a whole lot more sober than raves. Thanks to the aforementioned neo-Beats and the Pulp Generation, you can now wear wacky vintage clothes and chit chat over martinis in slick, ambient clubhouses. This is steaming kitsch, twice-reheated, and served to the goateed party in the corner booth.

Walking the city... L.A. has street life. You just need your car to get to it. Despite the griping of locals who want to see time stand still, all of these neighborhoods have been polished and made more user-friendly by eighties urban renewal: Santa Monica's Third Street Promenade, Old Town in Pasadena, Los Feliz at Hillhurst and Vermont, Silver Lake Boulevard around **Spaceland** (See The Club Scene), Franklin Avenue near **Bourgeois Pig** (see The Bar Scene), Santa Monica Boulevard's Theater Row, the very Martha Stewart Montana Avenue, Main Street near the beaches, the Sunset Strip, even Hollywood Boulevard. These city blocks anchor the entire urban sprawl, offering havens where you can not only drink, dance, and nosh but also hear poetry, see comedy, buy a book, and spill excellent expresso on your torn jeans. (See Hanging Out.)

Karaoke... It's not just for drunk salarymen anymore. L.A. has a way of taking camp so far beyond the pale that it becomes wholesome. In this age of ironic self-deprecation, we all—especially, it seems, the Asian, Chicano, and Anglo youth of Los Angeles—want to sing with the videos, putting on the mask of holy fool for our dates. (See The Bar Scene.)

Microbrews, single malts, and imported vodka... Drinking excellent beers and drop dead martinis. This is what being an adult is all about, right? So why limit yourself to standard issue Bud or a mixed drink that doesn't taste sinful? While microbrewery beers have brought class to local hops-heads, Nick and Nora wanna-bes discover the difference between High- and Lowland malts. (See The Bar Scene.)

Dance, swing, and retro clubs... Did dance clubs ever become passé? Not really, but now deejays have generations of material to work into the mix, and live bands pack in today's jitterbuggers. Best of all, you get to dress up, drink, and get all sweaty with strangers. (See the Club Scene.)

Hideo Nomo... The Dodgers' Japanese pitcher has brought a new Asian pride to the boys in blue. Dodger Stadium has never really gone out of style—not with its famous foot-long hot dogs, its organ player, and its hillside view of the Los Angeles basin. But with Nomo and an international squad drawing a diverse Pacific Rim crowd, Dodger Stadium is as close to a guaranteed good night as you'll find in town.

Pacific Rim pig-outs... For late night carbo-loading, nothing beats noodles, fish sauce, and Korean pickles. Whether it's Thai, Chinese, Japanese, or Korean, dozens of restaurants in Hollywood, downtown, and Koreatown stay open late and serve good eats, cheap. (See Late Night Dining.)

What's not

Big hair bands... The heyday is done. Eddie Van Halen has cut his hair, and the Strip behemoth Gazzarri's is closed. Still, ham-fisted rock, although outré, won't go away. Just check out the leather-clad fauna along Sunset around Guitar Center in Hollywood. (See The Club Scene.)

***Pulp Fiction* knock offs...** Like bad art, you can't describe it, but you know it when you see it. No one is immune, not even Quentin Tarantino. Around the bar at Hollywood's **Jones**, you may find yourself wondering if you should be ordering a Grand Royale with cheese. They'll give it to you, but just be warned, it's getting cold.

Urban cowboys... From line dancing to two-step, cowboy boots to rhinestones, the Western motif is deader than dead. The Palomino Club, the southern outpost for the Bakersfield–Fresno country music scene has closed, and L.A. is poorer for it. Fortunately, country swing is making a comeback; check out clubs like **Jack's Sugar Shack**. (See The Club Scene.)

Beverly Hills... It was always expensive and inane, but at least for a while in the eighties Beverly Hills had an over-the-top chic, what with its own Fiorucci store and a viable art gallery scene. Since the recession, nobody can afford anything in Beverly Hills, and not even "90210" can help. At night, the streets are empty. Where's Nancy Reagan when you really need her?

LOS ANGELES ⟨ WHAT'S HOT, WHAT'S NOT

the clu

b scene

Say what you want about
the smog, the drive-bys,
the earthquakes, the riots,
the fires, the endless
sprawl. Life in L.A. may
be hell, but at least it's got
a good soundtrack. Blues,

rap, swing, folk, jazz, country, lounge, industrial, techno, noise, bluegrass, unplugged to overamped, rock of every alternative perversion—there are as many styles as Tower has bins.

Scenes duplicate so quickly it's never easy to tell if you're at an authentic show or a clone of a scene that has long since vanished. Take today's swing scene, for example. When you see a room full of slick, twentyish hooligans dressed to the nines in pinstriped suits executing flawless lindys, you don't know whether you've wandered into a land of *Bladerunner*-like cyborgs or just had one too many. Is it hiply ironic or a strange consumer craze? Nobody cares. It's L.A. There is no history. Go with it. Clubs ride a wave of popularity and then vanish as suddenly as they appeared. Trends can race through the venues like grass through a goose, in and out of style before newly dyed hair has a chance to grow out. Big hair gives way to buzz cuts, tight leather to torn jeans, Southern Comfort to martinis. Although you may not trust their critics, the local free newspapers have the best information about what's coming up where.

Even though Hollywood calls itself the entertainment center of the world, the L.A. club scene was pretty provincial until a postwar jazz and R&B scene took root in small clubs in the black neighborhoods on Central Avenue. The musicians may have made their money playing for the studio execs at the Coconut Grove, but once the gig was over, they'd come down here to party. In the fifties it began to shift slowly to Hollywood, to the lounges and newly sophisticated bars on Sunset. Then came the sixties and all hell broke loose—the Doors at the Whisky, hippies naked in Elysian Park, riots on Sunset Strip. Party time! The seventies brought disco and a huge explosion of dance clubs, many in West L.A. and what is now West Hollywood. All the Soul Train dancers got their starts (and paid their bills) working the dance-contest circuit that promoters initiated to bring in the crowds. For musicians, it was still the Sunset Strip where things happened. Then along came punk in the late seventies, and nothing has been the same since. Punk promoters learned you could rent out a hall, Xerox some flyers, and without benefit of a permit, have a grand old time until the cops shut it down. Just about anything would pass, from a bowling alley to a barge in the Los Angeles Harbor. The Strip, now the home of the rock establishment, was anathema, and for a time punk was banned from Hollywood clubs, finding instead a friendlier reception downtown, in the South Bay area, even in East L.A. In the eighties, the big money on the Strip was in big-hair metal bands, the occasional art-damaged postpunk group, or the much safer (and sillier) new wave zoo. Gothic and gloom-doomed dance clubs started up around this time, often in old dance clubs or in the warehouses and Elks Club halls original-ly discovered by the punks, thus offering a respectible (or at least less guilty) version of the not live (but *not* disco!) dance music. By the end of the eighties, the scene had shifted all over the southland. Seeds sprouted in the the most unlikely places, sort of a second punk do-it-yourself revolution, only this time with better organization and the right permits. Old funky dives and bars could be rented out for a dance night, or leased and spiffed up with a fresh coat of paint and a new *très*-cool attitude. And guess what? There were a whole bunch of new kids just aching to have a scene of their own again. So it was, and one hopes, so it shall ever be.

Adult Entertainment

Just how nasty is Los Angeles? Well, our white-bread neigh-bor just over the hills, the San Fernando Valley, is thought to be the largest producer of pornographic videos and movies in the U.S., probably only because the studio rates in Hollywood are too high. Anyway, after dark is when you want to take your walk on the wild side. What do you want? Topless, nude, ama-teur nights, baths, sex shops, video arcades, peep shows? You want fries with it? Most of these unspeakables go on during the day for a reduced cover charge, but unless you're the sort that likes to sit in a dark bar at noon trying to stomach a non-alcoholic beer, you have to wait until the shadows fall. And no, seeing is not believing. About 13,000 breast augmentation operations take place in L.A. each year, and those dollar bills you give the strippers help keep our plastic surgeons employed, thank you.

The law in L.A. prohibits all-nude clubs from serving any alcohol. Fruit drinks, sodas, and nonalcoholic beers only, please. In all strip clubs, topless or all-nude, no physical con-tact between dancers and patrons is allowed, two drink mini-mums are common, and cover charges are high.

Sources

You can pick up *The Reader*, *The L.A. Weekly*, and *The Village View* just about everywhere. Overall, *The L.A. Weekly* has the best listings, especially in the dance catagory. And anything

LOS ANGELES ◡ THE CLUB SCENE

that their critics have highlighted is certain to be well attend-ed. The gay freebie *4-Front* also has good dance and bar list-ings, less comprehensive but totally up-to-date, and with a handy night-by-night format. For listings years in advance, check out the display ads in the Sunday "Calendar" section of the *L.A. Times.* Also in the *Times*, look for the "At the Clubs" column by Heidi Siegmund Cuda. For accuracy and true enthusiasm, she's the best in town.

Geographically, the endless sprawl means you have to know where you're going. A good map of the city is as impor-tant as the weekly music listings. Unlike more compact cities where clubs huddle together companionably, in L.A. there are just a few highly concentrated hot spots on the entertainment radar. Hollywood, downtown, the South Bay, and Santa Monica have played host to specific genres, splintering from one another but each providing a uniquely regional spin— Hollywood punk circa 1979, for example, was a lot more campy, flamboyant, druggy, and gay than its early eighties flannel-and-shaved-head counterpart from the south beaches. Now there's a gay and Latino-inflected dance scene in Silverlake and Los Feliz. On Pico Boulevard, and south of Hollywood on Santa Monica Boulevard, new scenes are sprouting, drawing clubgoers into previously unexplored areas of the city. The one constant in the club scene is its variety— and finding a parking space.

Getting Past the Velvet Rope

Getting into clubs is not a problem, generally. There's too much competition for club owners to use exclusivity as an artificial lure. Just as you can't judge a scene inside by the marquee on the street, no doorman can gauge the depth of a clubgoer's pockets by the cut of the trousers—although some certainly try.

Madonna's left. So has Roseanne. The streets are safe again. And face it, if you can't find a band, a deejay, or a comic to tickle your fancy on a weekend night in L.A., you should probably rent a movie and spare the world your tired old self.

The Lowdown

Best garage bands... Trying to name the best underground music outlets in a club-rich city like L.A. is a lot easier than you might expect—as long as you keep your demands simple: Interesting bands (signed or not), in intimate surroundings, casual yet competent staff, an audience free of cliques and pig-eyed drunks. Typical of L.A., the two best are on opposite sides of the city in areas not known as entertainment meccas: Echo Park and Culver City.

On a sleepy section of Silver Lake Boulevard, **Spaceland** is simply another of the seemingly endless pools for L.A.'s musical bottom feeders. It can't quite escape its former life as a disco. The sign outside says L.A. Dreams and inside it's all cheap, ugly modern, a sad attempt at upmarket decor, circa 1985. Such dreams have been replaced by the funkier and grittier reality of L.A.'s newer music. It's arguably one of the most influential and reliable places to see up-and-coming bands for whom the Major Label Contract is still just a dream (or nightmare). The crowd is largely young, hip, arty, ethnically diverse. Pretty much what the neighborhood is like. Young, razor-cut Hispanics, nerdish rock-crits, the girlfriend of the drummer in the band playing last—these are your barmates. The sight lines are great and the sound adequate. Forget the ho-hum alcohol selection, the lack of character in the setting. Spaceland's attraction is a wildly diverse booking policy that can be hit-or-miss, but the covers are low and if the first band is lousy, don't worry, the next one will be up in a few minutes. Meanwhile, on a funky section of Pico you'll find **Jabberjaw**, a mixed-media coffeehouse mosh pit. It's a tiny, concrete-floored misfit that belongs on any new-music lover's must-hit list. Think of it as our own little touch of Seattle. It would be hard to find a nightclub that has as much of a trendoid buzz to it as this tiny hole-in-the-wall. It's seen performances by some of the best unknown acts before they hit the big time: Jesus Lizard, Helmet, even pre-*Nevermind* Nirvana. Thrashed furniture, graffiti, and indie CDs for sale at the cash register make this an excellent bookend to Spaceland on the other side of town.

Alt.rock... It used to be that visiting alternative bands did the Sunset Strip, playing to crowds of industry operators curious to check out the out-of-town buzz. Either that, or bands like Sonic Youth would stage quasi-legal, guerrilla shows on warehouse loading docks downtown for crowds of tragically hip scenesters. Now good bands pop up in more mundane surroundings—like **The Alligator Lounge** on Pico, in the shadow of a freeway overpass. Formerly anonymous and soulless from the outside, the Lounge has recently gotten a face-lift to make it easier to find. Inside are red walls and a funky old roadhouse feel that harken back to its days as a major Cajun music outlet. There's Bass on tap, but the crowd comes for the music (Jonathan Richman, X, Thurston Moore, Frank Black, Noise Addict, Yo La Tengo, Cornershop) not the booze. This is the kind of place where household names come to bond with the fans. Think House of Blues with a nicer staff, a less pretentious audience, a cheaper cover, and easier parking. It's a friendly room with an eclectic bent. Much larger and with a slightly younger crowd is **Dragonfly**, a wonderfully inventive space that mixes warehouse-size dimensions with miles of billowing fabric draped just about everywhere. The stage is high, the sound good, and there's plenty of room to wander, from the throbbing dimly-lit dance room to a cushion-filled cubbyhole hallway called the Harem Room. The original idea was to create an "Egyptian bathhouse" atmosphere, a concept that seems to have been forgotten now. But no matter. Farther east there's the **Martini Lounge**, a space that is no stranger to L.A. clubbers. In its previous incarnation as The Grandia Room, it was a mainstay for the eighties postdisco, pretechno, hard-core dance scene. Now under the direction of Ava and Steve, a brother-sister team from Chicago who used to own the trend-setting '80s dance club Vertigo, the club has been reborn. There's a nice, large main room, oversize, bulbous black booths, a low, easy-to-see stage (live bands on Wednesdays and Thursdays) and a full kitchen. The music themes change during the week—reggae on Mondays, industrial on Tuesdays, salsa on the weekends—so the crowd shifts accordingly. But no matter what the music, the sound system is fantastic (the same brand as used for Woodstock '94 and the Monsters of Rock tour). If you're lucky enough to be following the right people, you'll find the entrance to Hollywood's up-and-coming **Opium Den**, down near the sound studios and production houses on Ivar. Look for bowling shirts, bike leathers, wing tips. You stroll down a long walkway and come into what looks like the basement of a rambling house. There are exposed rafters and brick, a blend of bombed-out and hasty rehab. It's a new place for Hollywood hipsters to hang or showcase their precious projects on the small stage. So new it's still trendy, so private it probably won't stay that way. It's got nothing in the way of character, but give it time. This is the latest project of scene maven Brent Bolthouse, who created Roxbury's notorious Saturday Night Fever. Not quite as happening as it was when it hosted seminal L.A. bands, like the Minutemen and Saccharine Trust, the anonymous **Anti-Club** is still trying to make things jump in a quiet, faraway corner of Melrose. It has a chain-link fence surrounding a bare-bones patio off the stage. They've redecorated; the covers are low or nonexistent, and live bands play only Thurday through Saturday. But check it out. Soundgarden once played here, and the Red Hot Chili Peppers, viewed by the punker-than-thou regulars as phony, used to be hooted off the stage. There's always hope.

Death by velvet cord... Let's pretend we love attitude. Give it value on par with talent. It's a hurdle that makes your night all the sweeter when you clear it. Who cares if you enjoy the music—just getting in the door is a battle won. What areas of L.A. have the most inbred attitudes? Beverly Hills and Hollywood, of course, homes respectively of **LunaPark** and **The Viper Room**. Working the tonier end is LunaPark, sitting on the very edge of Beverly Hills. It's a meandering, cavernous space, with a large main concert room upstairs and a far more intimate facility downstairs, in what should be a basement but works as a cozy place to nod out to jazz noodlings or get sweaty to a R&B band. The place is run with a European flourish by Jean-Pierre Bocarro, a transplanted Parisian, who in the eighties single-handedly transformed the term *cabaret act* from a pejorative into something almost respectable. If you're not dressed in expensive designer clothes, or have a face that's currently on bus-stop movie ads, you won't be able to get past the Neanderthal doormen when a name act is playing—you're likely to see everybody from a smokin' zydeco band to the next Coolio or the next Pearl Jam. They have excellent food, but the Eurotrash attitude will quite likely spoil your appetite. On the seedier side of the street is The Viper Room, actor Johnny Depp's vanity venue, much friendlier and way popular. When the club was known as The Central, it was a low-key blues and rock bar, one of the sleepier dives on the Sunset Strip, where you could quietly nurse a beer and enjoy so-so music without having to pay too much attention. Now, it's the slum du jour for rock celebs fumbling after roots they never had. For the highly-acclaimed superstar Monday-night jam sessions, only top-heavy models with major implant action and dudes with 'tude in $1000 leathers will make it past the door. Depp has added some nice Deco sconces to the bare-bones upstairs room, and presumably scraped off years of vomit. If you get inside, you'll probably have fun—if you can just get to the bar.

Los Angeles unplugged... It's not a club, but as one of the most respected stringed instrument retail stores in the city, **McCabe's Guitar Shop**, on a nondescript block in Santa Monica, is home turf for musicians, both local and visiting. And their cozy little performance space at the back has been presenting unplugged shows for years, long before MTV made it unhip. Shows happen Friday through Sunday only, and tickets can be bought in advance from McCabe's. The seats are uncomfortable, the room geared more to the comfort of the artists' works than the audience's butts, but never mind. It can be worth it to enjoy Ry Cooder or local hero John Doe of X on a solo night. And on your way out, be sure to pick up some strings for the dulcimer.

Legends in the smog... Two words, pal: the **Troubadour**. The list of famous names that have stumbled through these West Hollywood doors is too lengthy to consider—start with sixties folk rock and run all the way to the latest generation of metal bands and you get a small sampling. Let's just say that this tavern-style club in West Hollywood has seen its ups and downs. Now, after a fairly lengthy slumber as a pay-to-play stage, the club is again worthy of respect. The sound is good, and except for some cosmetic-rouge-colored carpeting, the decor has stayed the same for decades, with lots of stained wood and comfy seats both in the music room and out in the lobby. Drinks and covers are fairly priced. Anybody who would book the veteran British psychedelic dub band Dub Syndicate rates high with me.

And what would L.A.'s musical heritage be without the **Whiskey A Go-Go**? Like everything in L.A., it's seen better days but manages to reinvent itself periodically. It still is one of the best intimate clubs to see a band, slam headlong into sweaty strangers, and enjoy a companionable pukefest in the toilets. Black walls, black stage, cheesy silver tinsel hanging from the black ceiling, the place reeks of musical history and you feel like nothing has changed since the Doors were the house band in 1966. The sound is good, the upstairs balcony no longer closed off to the untrendy, and the booking policy has helped reestablish the place's street cred. The no cover Monday night shows—featuring a half-dozen bands you probably never heard of but might enjoy—is the best deal in town. Just up the street at **The Roxy**, the tables are small, closely packed, and the sight lines suck in some sections. Another Strip veteran with a mostly respectable past (depending on your musical politics), it was *the* industry showcase in the seventies and eighties, a place where labels picked up the bar tab and the trough was thick with geeky rock critics and record label middle-management burnouts. The charge accounts are gone, but the crowds still come. Playing host to everyone from the Boss to David Bowie, The Roxy is like the established older brother to its more rowdy sibling down the block. Covers vary depending on the talent.

Big, ugly discos... This is a big city, and so there's plenty of places to shake your booty with zillions of like-minded Travolta wanna-bes. First there's **The Strip**, on Friday nights only right now in the old Casablanca club, now named Club 8240. In this massive, 10,000-square-foot

LOS ANGELES ◟ THE CLUB SCENE

space, they attempt to bring something of Vegas excess to the Sunset Strip. Showgirls, deejays, bands, blackjack tables and, perhaps most important, five full bars where you can drink for a buck a shot all night. And to help you sober up, they also offer a free food buffet from 2 to 3am, when they close. On Saturdays, in the same cavernous space, there's something new about to begin called The House of Flesh, reportedly from the people who created a slew of other gothic, sex addict, rave-ish perversions with names like Stigmata and Fetish. We're talking the standard techno-alternative-industrial-house mishmash. But their motto is "undress to impress," which sounds intriguing. Then, across the street there's **Roxbury**, on three floors, complete with live music. But you'll come for the deejays, who spin everything from Dutch techno to trance to retro-funk. Don't miss the recent revival of popping and locking dance-offs. If 22,000 square feet of sweaty club kids packed into a former ice factory sounds like fun, try **Arena**. Open Thursdays through Sundays, the nights vary greatly in theme: deep house on Thursdays; techno and industrial on Fridays; Latin salsa and house on Saturdays; and on Sunday it's live Latin bands! One great dinosaur of the disco era still thriving is the **Florentine Gardens**, which has managed to survive the birth and death and rebirth of disco without losing a step. It's a massive place, a favorite safe first-date choice for young Latin club kids. Techno, progressive house, 160 bpm rave mania is standard. But on Thursdays, when live salsa comes in, you'd better know what you're doing before you get out on the floor. Thursday nights, salsa is the sound happening at the newly renovated **El Rey Theatre**. This historic landmark seats about a thousand, but why come if you're just going to sit and watch?

Dance fever... L.A. is the land of a thousand dances. OK, maybe not a thousand, but certainly too many to list here. It all depends on what sets your blood pumping. Industrial? By all means check out Kontrol Faktory at **The Probe**, held on Mondays. Gothic? Do you really dance to gothic music? Or just sort of relapse? Anyway, Helter Skelter is a Wednesdays-only night for the black-lipstick set, also held at Probe. Deep house is a fave genre for dance clubs all over the city, but I like it at **Hell's Gate** on Fridays because the place is so antidisco in tone that I don't feel guilty. Then there's that dance entity known as seventies retro. Are we talking disco or just recycled K-Tel classics? Don't even worry about it. Just come on by to the fountainhead of the genre that would not die at Saturday Night Fever on Saturdays (of course) at the otherwise overbearing **Roxbury**. Although alternative rock is not usually the stuff of dance-floor mania, promoter Dayle Gloria is making it work on Thursdays at Club With No Name at The Probe, mixing it up with the occasional live band. Gloria made an underground name for herself with her precedent-setting Scream back in 1989. Now, there's a new place to sneak out to on a Thursday night when you said you were going to the library. It's for all ages. Expect the odd kitsch classic like "Disco Inferno" thrown in for flavor. An interesting blend of techno-alternative-industrial takes over the next night at Stigmata, also at The Probe, on Fridays. Open way late. For the best, overall dance scene try Fridays at the **Love Lounge**.

Gem is an oddity—a dance club in the middle of Melrose's retail madness. It's narrow, has high ceilings, and feels like a former boutique (which it certainly was in one incarnation). They impose a velvet cord look-see here sometimes, depending on the crowd already inside, a silly attempt to create a buzz. I don't think so. Basically it's young kids, Euroweenies, and locals too drunk to drive to a real club. The music is so-so but the pickup scene is fab.

Best free dance party... The Toledo Show at **Union**, held every Monday and with no cover, has to be the best deal in town, featuring one of the city's best-known deejays. So what if there's really no room to dance? The large, cheap drinks and the feel of a Victorian pub-club that has seen better days are a perfect match. If you just gotta dance, go across the street to **Roxbury** and make a total ass of yourself where nobody will notice.

West side lounges with deejays... Maybe it's because of the earthquakes or the nearly unvarying climate, but there aren't very many underground venues in L.A. If you find yourself in Santa Monica one evening to check out the most glorious beach views in L.A., drop by **14 Below**. Despite the odor, there's a great feel here. Down the steps from the parking lot on 14th Street, you find out there is life beneath Santa Monica Boulevard. And it smells. The barroom at the entrance is cozy, warmed by a gas fire, and reeks of puke. "We can't find the cause [of the smell]," the bartender says when a patron asks why it always smells of vomit. "We steam-cleaned and everything." In the odor-free middle dance room a deejay spins some great hip-hop, while beyond is another room sporting three pool tables. Above ground and catering to a small but active local scene is **The West End**, a cozy place that feels like a former locals tavern—checkerboard, worn linoleum floors, old wooden bars that lots of bellies have rubbed against. Black-light strips are scattered throughout, most over the long bar in the high-ceilinged front room. The stage here is large and low, and the sound system strong enough to echo in your stomach. Low stress, zero attitude. That changes on Sundays when Doc Martin and other hot dance deejays take over the turntable. It really gets jumping for The Funky Hippieez, a retro-sixties dance band.

Eurotrash scenes... Like the lack of fall colors, sometimes the overabundance of Spanglish and flat Midwestern twang in Los Angeles can get to you, even out on the dance floor where you usually can't hear yourself think, much less talk. Fortunately there's **Louis XIV**, a bar-restaurant-dance scene on La Brea where, if you bum a cigarette, odds on you'll get a Gauloise. And everybody smokes here. Elegant Persian lads, sneering Parisians, slumming New Yorkers, rail-thin models. The music is techno-acid jazz, and the later it gets the louder it becomes. No torn jeans, please. Also consider **LunaPark**, where you at least get some good live music with the insulting staff. You can't help but dis the club for its eighties door policy, but they do some of the most interesting booking in town—live ambient, jazz, soul, world beat, and funk.

Good, clean fun for loft dwellers... Ever since the downtown loft scene began with artists, musicians, and other enemies of the status quo, **Al's Bar** has been the locals' clubhouse, playground, stage, and canvas. The interior has been revamped periodically, but basically in a downwardly mobile style. Two huge crossbars (forming a properly punkish X) could be a statement but are actually just earthquake struts. There's a nice pool table, which always seems to be in use, right next to the main bar; in the music room, there's nothing but the barest essentials—a few chairs, a square stage enclave, another bar for when it gets crowded. The walls are covered in layers of scribblings, doodles, graffiti tags, drawings. The covers, like the music, vary wildly. You don't necessarily come for the music, but for the gritty, downtown mood. Every neighborhood should have an Al's. Bonus point: It's next to *Booker's General Store* which has a fantastic selection of cigars.

For groovy ghoulies and kids with big hair... If your idea of L.A. nightlife means Hollywood, and *only* Hollywood, then **Hell's Gate** is the answer. With two rooms and its very own outdoor patio, there's a slightly creepy Gothic-Deco atmosphere, and a properly trashy mix of barflies and black-on-black fans. If the nightly live bands leave you cold, creep back past the bar and stare at the glassed-in collection of nightmare creatures, including snake tanks and aquariums with somehow familiar-looking piranhas. It's nice to know the Hollywood underground still has a home. **Bar Deluxe** (see The Bar Scene) offers a bit more of the same in only slightly upgraded surroundings. This is *real* Hollywood, something the Valley kids cruising on the Boulevard a half block away never see. If you like the Cramps you'll probably appreciate the bar-as-junk-shop, with a psycho-billy decor of black walls, animal skulls, and neon aquarium geegaws. It's hard to tell the artifacts from the patrons, who have lots of black leather, tattoos, and greasy hair. The stage on the recently renovated second floor is bigger now, but it's still a neighborly experience seeing music here.

If you think history began with Motley Crüe... The **Coconut Teaszer** was *the* hangout for the Hollywood trash-band scene. The hip, bastard child of the Strip scene that spawned Van Halen, it drew bands, fans, and lurking industry scouts through the eighties. There's still a bit of that presence around, but nothing like the overhyped vibe of days past. Which is good in some ways. The club's reverted to being a casual spot, with cheap drinks and interesting booking. Don't worry, there's always enough space to escape from that Swedish country-punk band. The performance room features low ceilings, mediocre sound, a tiny stage with irritating support beams blocking the view at strategic places, sawdust on the floor, and a full bar. Bonus point: The Crooked Bar downstairs, where there's never a cover, hosts an endless stream of wanna-be talents embarrassing themselves onstage.

For urban cowboys... It's not that **Jack's Sugar Shack** is so hard to find, just that it's a bit overwhelmed by the Hollywood tourist schlock all around it. It seemed much more like home when it was down on Pico, but at least it's still open. When the Valley's late, great Palomino closed down for good in 1995, finding roots country-swing-rockabilly in L.A. got harder. Fortunately, Jack's has taken up some of the slack. Just down the block from the landmark Capitol Records building, Jack's has a great selection of beers on tap, sawdust on the floors, and an ill-conceived Polynesian decor that tries to cover up traces of the Howard Johnson's it used to be. Booker Eddy Jennings (who used to run San Francisco's happening Haight Street I-Beam club) brings everything from blues to rockabilly onto his foot-high stage. A big drawback: no permit for a dance floor. Ronnie Mack's Barndance, a midweek night of rockabilly and country-swing, is deservedly packed. Come early. Stay late. Dance. What's the best use for an old bank building? Turn it into a venue for essential Cajun culture. That's what you'll find at **Fais Do-Do**. Somehow this club has brought a countrified sensibility and Delta feel to a former temple of Mammon. Covers are low, food is delightful, music is spicy. They also get high marks for the welcoming attitude of the staff.

If you like to jitterbug... It's L.A., 1947. The war is over, the boys are home and swing is in control, especially at **The Derby** in Los Feliz. If you've got a vintage zoot suit or just a thrift-store pair of spats, this is the place to show them off. Jitterbuggers rule here. The women have tattoos and nose rings and wear cocktail dresses, while the men have tattoos and nose rings and wear fedoras and padded suits. And everyone's drinking martinis in this blend of way-cool nineties meets way-cool forties. If you're eating, you can snag one of the booths with the velvet curtains to hide from the hoard. Otherwise, come early and score one of the seats around the huge oval bar. The only drawback at the bar is that you won't be able to see the great dancing in front of the small stage. It gets jammed on the weekends, so come early.

Clubbing al fresco... No matter how good the music is, eventually you have to breathe some fresh air. And thanks to our glorious unchanging climate (and the ever-changing smoking laws), patios are popular additions. The **Coconut Teazer**'s patio is delightful, large and open, a great place to watch big hair dinosaurs practice air guitar. The long **Dragonfly** enclosure, even with the gurgling fountain, feels a little like a prison yard. But it's a coed yard, so that helps *quite a bit*. And even good ol' **Al's Bar** has an outside "space." It doesn't quite rate patio status. Think of it as a fairly clean downtown mini-alley where you won't get mugged or step on a used spike. A tamer, pleasant outdoor patio can be found at the multiple-personality coffee lounge, **Highland Grounds**, off Melrose.

Corporate blues... There's one born every minute. The blues is the soundtrack for the underclass, but you won't find many of the toothless homeless crying in their beers at Dan Aykroyd's national chain, the **House of Blues**. With T-shirts and memorabilia, it's a shopper's paradise. The faux funky decor comes from an artist's palette with loving care and the eye of a high-end set designer—it almost evokes a Louisiana fish-fry shack. The outside is covered in weathered tin siding, the inside bedecked in the weirdest, most wonderful folk art possible. The sound is fabulous, the Cajun food quite good, and the parking attendants and door men brusque and coldly professional. Of course it's a hit, arguably being the best place in L.A. to see a big name artist without worrying about getting a scratch in your Lexus or a dent in your complacency. And despite the name, it's not limited to blues. Just about everything plays here except slam-bam punk and alternative rock. It's no surprise—they want tame audiences. Absurdly high cover prices also help deter the mosh nation.

Best bar art... You're waiting for the bartender, the band is playing behind you, and your mind's a blank. That's when you appreciate having something *different* to look at (other than the better-dressed couples around you). Thank the club gods for decor like the women's high heels and relief map of the world at the **Martini Lounge**, the various creepy reptiles trying to sleep through the noise at **Hell's Gate**, or the wonderful bottle-cap Americana folk art made by Jon Bok at the **House of Blues**. Nearly worth the price of admission.

Seven nights in hell... Mutant zombies have invaded L.A. Your assignment, should you choose to accept it, is to spend seven nights on the town, seeking out the hidden slime pits where the invaders hang, sipping martinis, talking real estate, and wondering why they can't get a date. Mondays, head for Art Nite Open Mike at **Largo Pub**. The name says it all. At least you won't see mimes. Tuesdays, you move just up the street to **Canter's Kibitz Room** for The Big Tuesday Night Jam. Best advice: Eat and run. Wednesdays it's acoustic night at **Molly Malone's** (see The Bar Scene), limited firepower but lethal all the same. Thursdays, it's getting dangerous: Perversion at **The Diamond Club**. It's for those 18 and over. Need we say more? Fridays you'll have to shell out too much money for an empty room at the **Crush Bar**. The place used to be the bar-lounge for the Hollywood Trailways bus station, and I think some of the ghosts are still around. Keep your back to the walls, they're too ugly to face. Saturdays you're back in Hollywood for High Society at the **Night Watch**. Be warned. "Proper attire required" says the flyer. Take the platinum card. On Sundays, it's **The Century Club** playing music for "urban lifestyles." Are they toying with us or what? Be afraid, slick back your ponytail, Binaca your breath, and be *very* afraid.

Cabaret cacophony... Exactly what is **Genghis Cantina**? Half restaurant (the Genghis Cohen Restaurant), half cabaret, this Hollywood oddity is definitely schizo. The eating area and the stage are separated by a bar, making the point that you can listen and drink or eat and talk. But you can't talk, eat, and listen at the same time. Singer-songwriters, who will never get famous and know it, strum original material every night of the week, hoping that some A&R person or a producer in the crowd will at least make them rich. The stage is small but all seats face it. The menu is massive—99 dishes at last count. There are scores more cabarets, but only a few rate a passing glance. One is the **Largo Pub** on Fairfax. The room is quasi-elegant, the furniture comfortable enough for lounging, the drinks as entertaining as the talent. It's a nice, cozy place to hear songs that someone else will be making a million off of in a few years. Across the street is **Canter's Kibitz Room**, an adjunct to Canter's Deli, the classic, old L.A. 24-hour hangout (see Late Night Dining). The room, a small cocktail lounge, is sometimes more entertaining than the music, and there's always the deli next door if you really need some chopped liver. What kind of music do they play in the rain forest? Cabaret, apparently. Entering the door at **Amazon,** you find your-self no longer near the Santa Monica bluffs but on some Disneylandish jungle ride with a faux waterfall behind the bar, fake tropical tree trunks, and an ersatz canopy of leaves over your head. The performers for the nightly shows sit up in the canopy on a small stage, like some sort of seraphim. We are in the People's Republic of Santa Monica here—no smoking, donation cans to save the rain forest scattered around, a rack filled with eco-concern pamphlets near the toilets. The Rainforest Action Network meets here (as you'd expect) on the first Monday of every month. There's a whole nother vibe happening at **Highland Grounds**. This always popular off-Melrose joint is like an eager-to-please puppy, trying to be a little bit of everything for everybody: restaurant, bar, cabaret, coffeehouse. It's the last two that work the best, making this larger-than-average space one of the more popular hangouts for java fiends and emerging singer-songwriters. There's a nice outdoor patio, shaded by towering eucalyp-tus trees and warmed by a square, open fire pit. The smok-ers sit out here, chatting and tuning their guitars as they wait their turn. Gen X slackers nurse their cappuccinos alongside art students working on their first goatees. Upstairs in the loft area, there's a CafeNet Internet termi-nal. For $2 you might get some guy practicing his jazz scales or the next Beck. Bonus point: The Jody Maroni Sausage Sandwich—it costs $7.75, but you won't have to eat for days.

All that jazz and blues... For a brief period in the late 1940s, L.A. was the Left Coast home to jazz. There was the Cotton Club (for whites only), the Capri Club, the

Swing Club, and the scene down on Central Avenue. At Central and 42nd, black culture boiled over, spilling into the Downbeat, the Oasis, the Last Word—clubs of legendary influence that are all history now. Blues and jazz has now spread throughout the city, available every night of the week. For the last 25 years, one of the most respected names in local jazz circles has been **The Baked Potato**, a session player's home away from home over the hills from Hollywood in Studio City. It's small, but its impact has been huge, its presence inescapable. Who's gigged here? Lee Ritenour, Larry Carlton, Sonny Terry, Flora Purim. The list goes on and on. Now there's a sister club open in Pasadena's Old Town, considered by locals to be the best local jazz club. Admittedly there's not much competition, but even if it were on Beale Street, the club would be a contender. It's located in the basement of a new building (and shouldn't all jazz clubs be in basements?) and has great sound and sight lines, even from the bar. It's a show-case-style room, a place where jazz, Latin, and blues musicians come to test their bands, record live albums, and generally hang out in an atmosphere that is supportive and laid-back. There is a sense of freedom here, of stretching the limits before a live audience (music industry skeptics steer clear). The crowd is as mixed as jazz itself—young, would-be session players sitting next to middle-aged CEOs and their wives next to college kids on dates. Culver City's **Jazz Bakery** treats jazz like chamber music—reverentially. It has fold-out chairs and world-class players. Over in Glendale, there's also a mini–jazz scene happening, despite the comatose neighborhood. **Club Déjà Vu** feels like an abandoned watering hole, barely hanging on only because there's nowhere else to drink nearby. But, actually, this shoe-box-size venue can surprise you. It shares a wall with a huge pool and a video arcade, separated only by a fake waterfall flowing over plastic windows; and while the setting doesn't exactly evoke Robert Johnson, I saw a crazed blues guitarist called Gas House Dave there who transported the club to the Delta. Drawback: It closes at 12:30—this is Glendale, after all. Bonus point: Miles of street parking. Across the street is another Glendale jazz outlet, **Jax**, a woody supper club that dishes up nonintrusive music to go with your steak.

All that jazz and business... Part supper club, part intimate jazz showcase venue, the **Cinegrill** is perfectly situated for music industry reps who want to see some high-quality music in comfortable surroundings with a plate of decent, overpriced grub on their plate (pastas and California cuisine mainly). No one ever questions an expense receipt from the Cinegrill because it is strictly business here. The decor is blahsville, the seats at the bar require a two-drink minimum (which is strictly enforced, young man), and if you can't make small talk about the art work on the CD package you're working on, you may feel left out. The sight lines and sound are good, the ambience and feel as cold as ice.

All that jazz and coffee... You can find jazz-tinged noodlings happening at various coffeehouse cabarets all over town, but it would be hard to find one with as much of a true vibe to it as **Fifth Street Dick's Coffee Company** in Leimert Park. For a tiny cover, you get to huddle upstairs in the loft and get an education in jazz that is totally unique—up close and personal, friendly, and open until 5am on the weekends. This place is legendary among musicians, and it's not hard to see why.

Primary blues... There's no arguing with the vibe at **Harvelle's**, aka "the home of the blues." The minute you step through the door, it does feel like you've entered some well-worn, but gracefully aging, Chicago honky-tonk. You don't even think about the fact that you're in Santa Monica until you get out on the tiny, crowded dance floor and realize nobody can dance. The drinks are reasonable, the sight lines so-so if you're sitting near the back, as the stage is only about 6 inches high. It draws a highly varied crowd—all races, ages, and economic backgrounds. The wall is covered with 8-by-10 glossies of people who have stopped by, everyone from blues legends to R.E.M. to Hall & Oates. This is a great place to see white folks stepping on each other's feet to the blues. There's no food, unfortunately. Bonus point: Sierra Nevada beer on tap. A relatively new (and welcome) addition to the local blues scene is **The Mint**. The top of the bar is metal, the red-leather stools at the bar are bolted down, and the stage is pushed against the back wall. It was probably a nasty alkie dive once, but when you look up at the ceiling over the bar and get lost in the layers upon layers of 45s, you realize there's a hip, ironic nineties sensibility at work. Only two beers on tap and a handful of tables, but when it gets jammed, it's hot, intimate, friendly, and sweaty. You don't care. This *is* a scene. At the edge of Beverly Hills, you'll find **The Bailey**, mainly a bar for expat Brits, but lately it's been hosting R&B and blues. No points for decor or size, but their choice of regulars (including the aforementioned Gas House Dave) is a plus.

On the pansexual front... Gay culture has provided a leading edge for nightlife in every city of the world since civilization began. Where the homo and hetero worlds mix, like the confluence of two rivers, some exotic wildlife gather. For example, Sin-o-matic, held on Saturdays at **Club 7969** in West L.A. This is polymorphous perversity to the nth degree. Gay, straight, spiky 'dos, shaved heads, dancers who lead their partners with leather straps attached to dog collars. Up on the stage, two guys in thongs are dancing with a woman in a see-through blouse. Lots of posing goes on right in tempo to the almost lethal bass thumping out of the sound system. Don't worry about what you wear (or don't wear) here—just dress for sex. It'll pass. For ladies only, there's Michelle's XXX Review, a strip show for the butch in all of us, Tuesdays, also at Club 7969. It's a similar theme, different sexual orientation, at **Gauntlet II** on Thursdays, for the wet underwear contest. Fridays, it's Cherry at the **Love Lounge** in Beverly Hills, considered by many to be the best dance club in the city, thanks in large part to the inspired tastes of deejay and scene maker Joseph Brooks. The same night, in a far less tony location, there's Hai-Karate!, held at **Garage**, a shoe-box-size space that can barely contain the hormones exuding from the crowd. Saturdays, you don't sleep, heading for **The Probe** and its all-night theme parties that run until it's time for church on Sunday. And after church, it's back to Garage for Sucker, the late afternoon–evening "punk rock beer bust" hosted by the stately Vaginal Davis. And finally, it's back to West Hollywood on Mondays, to **Rafters**, an old-time cruising bar that is notable only for its Gay Bingo Night. Too weird to be missed.

Drag and beyond... Drag queens and cross-dressers are part of the multimedia mix in L.A., a viable alternative to the straight world. The crowds are mixed, the mood festive, the performers over-the-top. For example, there's Dragstrip 99 at **Rudolfo's** in Silverlake. It only happens once a month, on the second Saturday, but word of mouth has made this drag show–cum–dance club a superpopular event. You may not get in. But if you do, the mixed crowd and candy-glam stickiness should keep you going until they kick you out. An easier entry, but a similar mood can be found at Club Gloria, Tuesdays at Tommy Tang's restaurant on Melrose, in the **Tiki Ti** lounge. It's less a show per se than a séance invoking the spirit of your favorite, dead screen queen. The food is delightful—nouvelle Thai, low-fat, and heart friendly—but the seasoning for the entertainment is 100 percent Hollywood. At **The Plaza** on La Brea, cross-dressing is taken to new heights with a Latino drag show. The place is slightly down-at-the-heels, but no one cares, especially the mixed audience, which may include some families.

Topless bars... Where to begin? The topless scene has newfound cachet with the youth of today. Far from pandering to dirty old men, stripping is a pro-sex feminist assertion of independence—or so many Gen Xers who read Camille Paglia will tell you. Easily the hippest strip-bar dive in the city has to be **Jumbo's Clown Room**, a 25-year-old topless bar that offers a touch of sin with a safe, welcoming nonsleazoid ambience. The women who run the place are friendly and pleasant, and there's no cover. In many ways it's the perfect neighborhood bar plus something extra. It's hidden in a little run-down minimall along a particularly seedy section of Hollywood Boulevard; surrounded by Thai restaurants and grocery stores, laundromats, and a transients hotel, the area doesn't feel dangerous, just a little tired and frayed at the edges, kind of like Jumbo's itself. Despite its age, the bar consistently gets raves, most recently from *Details* in their 1995 "Sex" issue, the *L.A. Reader*, and even the *L.A. Times*. It's being touted as the next **Dresden Room** (see The Bar Scene), the sort of hype that would probably kill a place of lesser character or more shallow roots. The music is way above average. In a similar vein though lacking the history is **Cheetah's**, another neighborhood bar that also happens to have topless dancers, great music, and zero sex-on-sale vibes. It's a fairly new addition to the east side scene but

LOS ANGELES ◯ THE CLUB SCENE

just a few minutes drive from the bars and clubs on Vermont (Dresden Room and Amok) and Hillhurst (**The Derby**, **Good Luck Club**, **Vida**—see The Bar Scene), so it gets a healthy spillover of both locals and young trendoids—the tattooed, pierced, and couldn't-care-less. Date safe, you get a touch of the risqué without soiling your soul. Again there's no cover, no sleazy atmosphere, no lap dances, and men and women of varying sexual preferences. There's even a pool table. The fact that there are topless dancers on the small stage near the door seems totally incidental. In a former incarnation, this space was (briefly) a happening live-music dive, and it retains an underground vibe. The soundtrack runs from Nine Inch Nails to jackhammer punk.

A touch of burlesque... The venerable **Body Shop** is a weak but valiant attempt to fit the extravaganza of the Follies Bergère onto a tiny Sunset Strip stage. It doesn't really work, but this is the last true burlesque show in the city so it's definitely of historical value. The club has been here 40 years—a landmark by L.A. standards—and is the city's oldest strip joint. A big disco ball spins endlessly overhead, throwing sparkles through machine-made fog onto the inevitable red-and-black decor. It's comfortable, cozy, serves decent food, and looks much nastier from the outside than it actually is. The dancers have full routines worked out, with special effects, costume changes, and duets onstage, though the tiny stage doesn't really give the artistes room to strut their stuff. Popular for dates, the Body Shop is less about sex than the vaudevillian roots of burlesque: no lap dancing, no couch crunches.

Nude bars... Just a stone's throw from the concrete banks of the L.A. River in Silverlake, **Star Strip II** is totally nude. No pretense, no tease, no show. Oh, and no alcohol either, so fuzzy-cheeked 18-year-olds are plenty welcome to belly up next to the older oglers at the rail. Formerly known as Extasy, the change in name hasn't improved the clientele or the mood. It's small, adequately lit, and none of the dancers appear to be nodding off. Located in an industrial strip underneath a freeway overpass, you can sneak in here without worrying about anyone you know seeing you. The sister club on La Cienega, **Star Strip** is a more upscale affair. It's larger, boasts thick casino-style carpets, has eight stages, worse lighting, and a largely foreign audience that just got off the XXX tour bus. Actors from the porn-video industry reportedly come here on a busman's holiday. I doubt it somehow. **The Seventh Veil** is different from its peers only in the noticeably seedier ambience. The two drink minimum is strictly enforced, the cover charge is high, and if you come out of there not feeling like a freshly shorn sheep, you're kidding yourself. There are two stages, decent lights, and again, lots of foreign tourists, who can only be forgiven since they don't know any better.

If you like mud wrestling... Gee, wouldn't it be exciting to see a couple of babes in skintight bodysuits pushing each other around in a mound of mud? Well, maybe. Think camp, not creeps. Many (gainfully employed) couples report that mud wrestling, in its sheer Russ Myers–style excess, beats local comedy clubs, er, hands down for laughs per minute. If this meets your criteria for a night on the town, then **The Hollywood Tropicana** is for you. Perched nearly on top of the Hollywood Freeway in a cavernous space decorated in faux glitz, this space is reminiscent of the worst off-the-Vegas-strip hellhole. Add the totally bizarre, carnivalesque take on sexuality, and you've got a full evening of shame. The women get auctioned off by a barker who prowls the room, coercing the patrons to volunteer (and pay) for the opportunity to either manage a wrestler or to climb into the ring with one. Be forewarned that the covers are high, the drinks lousy.

What's so funny?... That's the question a lot of Angelenos ask themselves in between disasters. And if the disaster is the comic onstage, well, at least the drinks are big. There are just a handful of reliable comedy clubs, and considering the wealth of talent in town, you'd think they were all pretty equal. Not true, unfortunately. **Igby's Comedy Cabaret** in Culver City is spartan and has the feel of a converted disco, complete with a large mirror ball hanging lifeless from the ceiling. The sight lines are good, the stage small, the laughs hit-and-miss. Megastars, like Robin Williams and Bobcat Goldthwait, may stop by to work on a set in the low-pressure atmosphere—or you may get a nervous novice stumbling through a set that has you squirming in embarrassment. That's true at all comedy clubs, especially on midweek nights. Igby's has been the location for comedy tapings by Showtime, HBO, Comedy Central, and Cinemax, among others, but mainly it's a place to see young turks still raw and fresh before they hit the big-name clubs.

Before it became a retailer's zoo, the only reason to drive down Melrose at night was **The Improvisation**, where you could catch outrageous comics before they toned down their acts for national TV. However, The Improv lost the war with its cousins on the Sunset Strip (the winner was the Strip's Comedy Store), but still the crowds pack this place. Maybe it's the food—which is above the standard mush. You have more laughs outside in the entrance area. The prices are on the high side, the comics slightly less so.

The Laugh Factory used to be the office of Groucho Marx, but he wouldn't recognize it now. Its faux-window–backed stage, red booths, and chairs too close for comfort are a little over-the-top for comedy. It's comfortable, as long as it's not too crowded. The crowd is younger and hipper than at more high-profile clubs, and the music is appropriately louder. The club has seen more than its share of rising stars and, thanks to the philanthropic work of founder Jamie Masada, an Israeli comic, a fair amount of them return to pay back early support. The *Washington Times* called it "L.A.'s hippest comedy club," but is that a recommendation? If you're afraid of becoming a target for a comic, take a seat in the upstairs balcony area. Smack in the heart of the Sunset Strip is Mitzi Shore's **The Comedy Store**, still the queen on the laugh circuit even after a boycott by comics in the eighties, resulting in *mucho* bad press. A few years later, a lot of those striking turned up to celebrate the club's 20th anniversary in 1992—and with good reason. You'll get more bitter invective spewing from this stage than from years of riding New York subways. Guilty pleasures abound, and the talent is first-rate. The veterans from the stage here are a Who's Who of the country's best-known comics, including Garry Shandling, Robin Williams, Whoopi Goldberg, Roseanne, the Wayans brothers, Richard Pryor, Sandra Bernhardt, and, well, you get the idea. The Main Room feels like a Vegas lounge, very comfortable and dark, while the Belly Room (for female comics) is cozy and supportive. One of the few comedy clubs where you don't have to be drunk to think something's funny.

For older night owls... And don't think that you have to be 23 and rife with disposable bucks to have fun. L.A. is a city that is in serious self-denial when it comes to aging—just get a liposuction and a facelift—but that doesn't mean you can't have fun if you don't know jungle from techno. When I need a major jolt of maturity, I go to the **Atlas Bar & Grill**. It's large, well-appointed, has fantastic sculptures, a big-band scene (that plays salsa as well), and one of the best bars in the city. They call me sir. I like it. Also consider **The Baked Potato**, **Harvelle's**, **Catalina Bar & Grill**, or any of the comedy clubs.

My favorites... There are some places in L.A. where I always have fun, no matter what's going on, live music or not. My personal top five are **Union**, for its anti-Strip ambience; **Spaceland**, for its do-it-yourself street vibe; the **3 of Clubs** (see The Bar Scene), for the cozy atmosphere and menu of single malts; **Dragonfly**, for the nonstop circus atmosphere; and the legendary **Al's Bar**, a home away from home, for aging gracefully.

The Index

Al's Bar. Venerated by loft-living locals, comfy as a paint-splattered pair of jeans, this is one place that keeps changing but stays the same. Downtown life at its best: funky, cheap, covered in graffiti. Anything live here is cutting edge.... *Tel 213/625–9703. 305 S. Hewitt St., Downtown. Cover charge sometimes.*

The Alligator Lounge. Not much in the way of atmosphere, but the booking policy is one of the most experimental in town, anything from minimalist jazz to more mainstream household names. Great sound system and sight lines.... *Tel 310/ 449–1844. 3321 Pico Blvd., Santa Monica. Cover charge.*

Amazon. This is probably the most PC club I've ever experienced, the perfect place I'd want to bring my recently laid-off lumberjack buddies, now slapping burgers at McDonald's. Cabaret music in the clouds.... *Tel 310/394–2348. 307 Santa Monica Blvd., Santa Monica. Cover charge.*

Anti-Club. Back in the punk days of the late seventies and early eighties, this was a source for indie bands who couldn't get gigs anywhere else. Experimental, noisy, and funky, it's changed direction several times but is trying now to come back as an alternative spot. It's not there yet but is worth a look if the cover is under $5.... *Tel 213/661–3913. 4658 Melrose Ave., Hollywood. Cover charge sometimes.*

Arena. This is a huge space, a converted ice factory that now hosts a microview of what L.A.'s dance scene is all about: deep house, disco, industrial, techno, tribal, Latino genres of music, drag shows. Be prepared to sweat.... *Tel 213/ 462–0714. 6655 Santa Monica Blvd., Hollywood. Open Tue, Thur–Sun. 18 and over. Cover charge.*

Atlas Bar & Grill. A beautiful bar, good Caribbean-Californian cuisine, and a quirky, yet timeless decor makes this a great place to hear music (swing, jazz, salsa), have a drink before a concert at the Wiltern Theater (which is next door), or simply admire the huge sculptures hanging from the ceiling. One of the highlights of the Miracle Mile district.... *Tel 213/380–8400. 3760 Wilshire Blvd., Miracle Mile. Cover charge sometimes.*

The Bailey. Ignore the palm trees outside, the fake flowers on the wall, the strictly–L.A. cushy chairs and mirrors—this blend of dance club and Irish pub seems to work, evoking the loudest and most party-oriented of both worlds.... *Tel 310/275–2619. 8771 W. Pico Blvd. (at Robertson), L.A. Cover charge sometimes.*

The Baked Potato. Here's another reason to go to Pasadena: One of the best live jazz outlets in the entire city. Reliable, comfortable, intimate; hosts local and touring fusion, Latin, R&B, bebop, and straight-ahead performers. Plus great potatoes from their full kitchen.... *Tel 818/564–1122. 26 E. Colorado Blvd., Pasadena. Closed Mon. Cover charge.*

Body Shop. An old-school strip joint and the last place in L.A. to see burlesque.... *Tel 213/656–1401. 8250 Sunset Blvd., West Hollywood. Cover charge.*

Canter's Kibitz Room. Canter's 24-hour deli is next door, for years a musicians' after-hours hangout. The Kibitz Room is basically a fab fifties-style bar with singer-songwriter accessories. Covers vary, depending on quality. Sound sucks, but if you're sitting near one of the windows you get an aquariumlike view of the deli—which is often more entertaining than the live acts.... *Tel 213/651–2030. 419 N. Fairfax Ave., Fairfax. Cover charge.*

Catalina Bar & Grill. This is one of the most reliable and popular jazz clubs in town. Great sight lines, impeccable sound, a little too much attitude from the staff. Want to pass your demo to a record executive? This is the place to be.... *Tel 213/466–2210. 1640 N. Cahuenga Blvd., Hollywood. Cover charge.*

The Century Club. Big, full of marble and antiqued wood, this is a dance club (with live music as well) for those folks who never head east of La Brea. Lots of suits, rich foreigners, security bouncers wearing headsets. The sound system is great, the audience a big yawn, the drinks way overpriced. It's in Century City. What else could you expect?... *Tel 310/ 553–6000. 10131 Constellation Blvd., Century City. Cover charge; no cover Thur.*

Cheetah's. A topless bar that passes itself off as a neighborhood bar. Big with alienated youth coming home from nearby nightspots.... *Tel 213/660–6733. 4600 Hollywood Blvd., East Hollywood.*

Cinegrill. A good room with a snooty attitude and excellent talent that deserves better. You'll get legendary acts in your face, and music-industry execs, producers, and musicians as neighbors. Dress nice, tip well, drop names, and you'll have a great time.... *Tel 213/466–7000. Inside the Roosevelt Hotel, 7000 Hollywood Blvd., Hollywood. Cover charge, two drink minimum at bar.*

Club Déjà Vu. Jazz in Glendale? Blues in Glendale? Remarkably enough, both can be found on sleepy Brand Boulevard. There's no cover and a relaxed vibe at this odd little bar. If the music doesn't move you, take your drink into the pool room next door.... *Tel 818/547–3947. 224 N. Brand Blvd., Glendale.*

Club 7969. On Saturdays, host to Sin-o-matic, a pansexual dance club that should reawaken those hormones and may cause you to do something you'll seriously regret the next day. Tuesday brings Michelle's XXX Review for ladies only.... *Tel 213/654–0280. 7969 Santa Monica Blvd., West Hollywood. Cover charge.*

Coconut Teaszer. Once the home of the hottest up-and-coming Hollywood trash bands, the Teaszer is quieter now, but still wins points for the spacious layout and a free downstairs performance room, The Crooked Bar. Low ceilings, lousy sight lines, but a fabulous patio when the heat and smoke are too much.... *Tel 213/654–4773. 8117 Sunset Blvd., Hollywood. Cover charge; no cover for Crooked Bar.*

The Comedy Store. Probably the best surefire choice for a night of no-name comedy, this is the premier comics showcase in L.A. It's high visibility, so you probably won't get name-brand goofs working out their kinks before an overly appreciative crowd. The high cover on weekends is worth it.... *Tel 213/656–6225. 8433 Sunset Blvd., West Hollywood. Cover charge.*

Crush Bar. Once a happening scene, this weekends-only retro-scene somehow manages to keep going, playing good sixties soul and bad seventies disco.... *Tel 213/463–7685. 1743 N. Cahuenga Blvd., Hollywood. Cover charge.*

The Derby. This is nostalgia with a modern twist, a nightclub that reworks the past without being campy. The clientele dresses forties and fifties sharp, the music is impeccable, and if you can't jitterbug, just stand back, sip your martini, and watch. On weekends it gets packed.... *Tel 213/663–8979. 4500 Los Feliz Blvd., Los Feliz. Cover charge.*

The Diamond Club. This club is the current home of several notable dance nights, pushing the envelope of what's happening out on the floor. House, industrial, alternative, techno, and weird videos set the tone. The club is open nightly but come by on Thursdays for Perversion.... *Tel 213/467–7070. 7070 Hollywood Blvd., Hollywood. Cover charge.*

Dragonfly. Among the top five rooms in L.A., this is a fabulous place to dance, check out the newest bands, or just sink into the pillows in the Harem Room. Interior decor is dreamy, yet weathered, the clientele savvy to new music— which is why it's a hangout for major-label talent scouts. A great, high stage and a long outdoor patio to retreat to. Even if you don't know the band playing, you'll have a good time here.... *Tel 213/466–6111. 6510 Santa Monica Blvd., Hollywood. Cover charge.*

El Rey Theatre. A historic landmark that recently got a new dance floor, this is swing central on the first Friday of the month.... *Tel 213/936–4790. 5515 Wilshire Blvd., Miracle Mile. Cover charge sometimes.*

Fais Do-Do. This is the closest you'll get to Cajun country in L.A. Good food, nice people, great zydeco.... *Tel 213/954–8080. 5257 W. Adams Blvd., Los Angeles. Cover charge.*

Fifth Street Dick's Coffee Company. It's a coffeehouse for jazz freaks, legendary among musicians, and the most genuine outlet for roots riffs you'll find in L.A. The space is small, so the music is right in your face where it belongs.... *Tel 213/296–3970. 3347½ W. 43rd Place, Los Angeles. Cover charge.*

Florentine Gardens. A veteran cavernous space that is a coming-of-age site for young dance kids, a safe and anonymous place to take a date and not have anyone make fun of your steps.... *Tel 213/464–0706. 5951 Hollywood Blvd., Hollywood. Open weekends only, until 3am on Fridays, 5am on Saturdays. Cover charge.*

14 Below. We're below ground here, but you'd never know it. Three rooms rambling one into another, a long, narrow dance room, and a bar area that feels more like a pub than a cave, this is one of Santa Monica's more casual hangouts. Not for the claustrophobic.... *Tel 310/451–5040. 1348 14th St., Santa Monica. Cover charge sometimes.*

Garage. Boxy, small, and spare in character, this former gay bar has become a hot hangout of late. The music is great, the crowd is mixed, and it's right across the street from Jay's Jayburgers.... *Tel 213/667–9766. 4519 Santa Monica Blvd., Silverlake. Cover charge sometimes.*

Gauntlet II. A gay leather bar, more camp than serious.... *Tel 213/669–9472. 4219 Santa Monica Blvd., Silverlake.*

Gem. The attempt to transplant a forties-era nightclub to a storefront in the Gen X ghetto of Melrose's shops and boutiques is only a partial success. The club is small—two rooms—and has the requisite comfortable sofas and chairs, facing a long, copper bar. It gets packed, and it's fun and sweaty out on the dance floor but hardly such a scene that there should be a velvet rope mentality.... *Tel 213/932–8344. 7302 Melrose Ave., West Hollywood. Cover charge.*

Genghis Cohen Restaurant and Cantina. Mainly a pricey Chinese restaurant, the Cantina side gets most of the attention. It's a landmark on the singer-songwriter circuit, a definite step up from the standard coffeehouse, linoleum-floor stage. The seating area for the Cantina is narrow and limited, but the bar has nine different vodkas, so who cares?.... *Tel 213/653–0640. 740 N. Fairfax Ave., Hollywood. Cover charge.*

Harvelle's. It doesn't get much more down-home than at this 65-year-old Santa Monica landmark. People come to dance to the best blues in town, presented in a way intimate atmosphere. Another reason to move to the beach.... *Tel 310/395–1676. 1432 Fourth St., Santa Monica. Cover charge.*

Hell's Gate. Not all the snakes are behind glass at this seedy dive. Some are on the minimalist stage upstairs, others on the bar stools next to you. Dark, dank, and 100 percent genuine, this is the absolute belly of the Hollywood beast. Dress down, drink deep, and think black. You haven't been to Hollywood unless you pass through Hell's Gate.... *Tel 213/463–9661. 6423 Yucca St., Hollywood. Cover charge.*

Highland Grounds. You can get drunk on cheap, decent beer or wine or jacked up on espresso. How you digest the highly varied stream of more-or-less unplugged performers is another question. Low covers, intimate perspectives, this is a great place to sample coffeehouse culture, L.A. style. Has CafeNet terminal.... *Tel 213/466–1507. 742 N. Highland Ave., Hollywood. Open till 12:30 Tue–Thur, till 1 weekends. Cover charge sometimes.*

The Hollywood Tropicana. Mud wrestling. Need we say more?.... *Tel 213/464–1653. 1250 N. Western Ave., Hollywood. Admission charge.*

House of Blues. It's the Pirates of the Caribbean on the Strip. Slightly overpriced, great folk-art decor, a comfortably mainstream booking policy. The food is great, the seating comfortable, and the sound top rate. It's safe, not exactly surprising, but still a good spot to catch world music and blues acts....*Tel 213/650–0247. 8430 Sunset Blvd., West Hollywood. Cover charge.*

Igby's Comedy Cabaret. Laid-back in atmosphere, intimate in mood, this is one of the few name comedy outlets on the west side. Talent is sketchy, but the turnover is fast and the covers low.... *Tel 310/477–3553. 11637 W. Pico Blvd., West L.A. Cover charge.*

The Improvisation. The comedy room is tiny but the talent that graces the stage can be enormous. Jerry Seinfeld, Robin Williams, Jay Leno have all swung through, back in their salad days as unknowns and more recently for short, un-announced appearances.... *Tel 213/651–2583. 8162 Melrose Ave., West Hollywood. Cover charge.*

Jabberjaw. Spartan, weathered, and real. Yes, it's a coffee-house. But it's significance to the L.A. music scene, partic-ularly punk and underground, is way out of proportion to its size. No age limit. No alcohol. Their live-music schedule varies greatly, so call ahead.... *Tel 213/732–3463. 3711 W. Pico Blvd., Los Angeles. Cover charge.*

Jack's Sugar Shack. Country-swing, blues, and roots rock are alive and well in Hollywood, thanks to Jack's. There is an attempt to give a beach feel with palm fronds and sawdust on the floors, but it's a failed effort because of the neigh-borhood and its busloads of tourists. You have to rely on the music and fans to provide the ambience. Best bet: Ronnie Mack's Barn Dances on Tuesdays.... *Tel 213/466–7005. 1707 N. Vine St., Hollywood. Cover charge sometimes.*

Jax. It feels more like a restaurant than a jazz club but don't let the decor fool you. Even though there's no stage per se, the music is taken seriously—jazz, blues, whatever. There's no cover.... *Tel 818/500–1604. 339 N. Brand Blvd., Glendale.*

Jazz Bakery. It's more a concert hall than a club and it has zero ambience, being located within the former Helms Bakery complex in Culver City. But it's become one of the best places in the city to regularly see serious musicians work out serious licks. Probably the most uncomfortable seats outside of the Third World.... *Tel 310/271–9039. 3233 Helms Ave., Culver City. Cover charge.*

Jumbo's Clown Room. One of the oldest and, for many, best topless bars in town. It's clean and unassuming.... *Tel 213/666–1187. 5153 Hollywood Blvd., Hollywood.*

Largo Pub. Even though it made its name as a cabaret–spoken word venue, the Pub is now bringing them in for the bar, which is large and sophisticated, a nice place to have a mixed drink and chat. The room is comfy, and if there is someone decent working the stage, at least the sound is good.... *Tel 213/852–1073. 432 N. Fairfax Ave., Fairfax. Cover charge sometimes.*

The Laugh Factory. A nice, large room, nice, large drinks, and a moderate cover charge, here you'll get comedy free of bile in comfortable surroundings. Safe, yet still containing surprises over an evening, it's kind of like shopping at the mall—maybe you'll find something, maybe not.... *Tel 213/656–1336. 8001 Sunset Blvd., Hollywood. Cover charge.*

Louis XIV. Dark, smoky, with excellent Provence-style cuisine (if it ever arrives on your table), this is a little touch of the Left Bank on La Brea. Techno and jazz blast from the speakers, and everyone's smoking, drinking way good wine, gossiping about the rag trade in a mishmash of Eurobabble, and rating the clothes at the next table.... *Tel 213/934–5102. 606 N. La Brea Ave., Los Angeles. Cover charge sometimes.*

Love Lounge. On Friday nights, home of what many call the best dance club in the city: Cherry. A glam-slam evening for glitter guys and gals of all sexual persuasions.... *Tel 310-659–0472. 657 N. Robertson Blvd., West Hollywood. Cover charge.*

LunaPark. There's so much room at this elegantly designed club that you'd think they could be just a tad more pleasant to their clientele. Good food.... *Tel 310/652–0611. 665 N. Robertson Blvd., West Hollywood. Cover charge.*

McCabe's Guitar Shop. A west-side institution, the best place to see hip acoustic takes on country and folk. McCabe's sells tickets over the phone.... *Tel 310/828–4497. 3101 Pico Blvd., Santa Monica.*

Martini Lounge. Thick, velvet curtains separate a very nice bar from the dance and live-music area. Great cartoon-size booths you'll get lost in. No cover Mondays.... *Tel 213/467–4068. 5657 Melrose Ave., Los Angeles. Cover charge.*

The Mint. This funky dive on Pico is small but delightful, a great place for blues. Call for bookings; the schedule is irregular.... *Tel 213/954–9630. 6010 W. Pico Blvd., Los Angeles. Cover charge.*

Night Watch. This 19th-floor restaurant and dance club is home to four varying nights of rhythm, starting with salsa and funk on Tuesdays and winding up with funk, acid, and house during High Society on Saturdays. There is a "stylish attire" dress code.... *Tel 213/871–2995. 6290 Sunset Blvd., Hollywood. Open Tue, Thur–Sat. Cover charge; no cover with dinner reservation.*

Opium Den. This featureless hole-in-the-wall in Hollywood is so new it doesn't have much character yet.... *Tel 213/466–7800. 1605 Ivar St., Hollywood. Cover charge.*

The Plaza. It's dark, stinks of spilled drinks and sweat, crowded with hipsters, old and young, Latino and Anglo, gay and straight. But it's the talent that brings you back, drag performers with *très*-L.A. roots. Where else could you see Donna Summer in Spanish?... *Tel 213/939–0703. 739 N. La Brea Ave., Los Angeles. Cover charge.*

The Probe. A gothic yet flavorless venue. If you didn't have anything better to do, you could spend seven nights here and get a very complete idea of what goes in the L.A. dance scene. Originally a gay dance club, it's now open to everyone, though men shouldn't be surprised if they get cruised by other men on Saturdays. Mondays you'll find the Kontrol Faktory, an industrial dance club. Black on black is de rigeur Wednesdays for Helter Skelter, where you can zombie out to gloom music until 3am. The self-proclaimed Club With No Name, a one-nighter Thursdays, is cheap, has an undergroundish flavor, but is so new it could change (or die) quickly. On Fridays, Stigmata mixes and matches techno, industrial, and alternative. Best of all, it lasts until 4am.... *Tel 213/461–8301. 836 N. Highland Ave., Hollywood. Cover charge.*

Rafters. Basically a gay cruise bar circa 1975, the big reason to come is their Gay Bingo Night on Mondays.... *Tel 213/654–0396. 7994 Santa Monica Blvd., West Hollywood.*

Roxbury. About the only reason to visit this monstrosity is the long-lived Saturday Night Fever, dedicated to everything you sneered at 10 years ago.... *Tel 213/656–1750. 8225 Sunset Blvd., West Hollywood. Cover charge.*

The Roxy. No longer the industry hot spot it once was, but it still can surprise you. Good sound, but none of the street vibe that makes its neighbor The Whiskey, much more fun. No age limit. Free on Tuesdays for 21 and over.... *Tel 310/276–2222. 9009 Sunset Blvd., West Hollywood. Cover charge.*

Rudolfo's. It's small, has a nice patio, but may be a little too close to the freeway. Salsa, alternative bands, and on the second Saturday of every month, Dragstrip 99, a drag show and dance club and the hottest special event (as well as one of the hardest to get into) on the east side. Can you say that about your local family Mexican restaurant?... *Tel 213/669–1226. 2500 Riverside Dr., Silverlake. Cover charge sometimes.*

The Seventh Veil. An overpriced all-nude club, best left to the busloads of tourists who crowd it.... *Tel 213/876–4761. 7180 Sunset Blvd., Hollywood. Cover charge, two drink minimum.*

Spaceland. Totally unpredictable, completely attitude-free, this unpretentious converted disco is the cheapest and best place to see what's fermenting in the L.A. unsigned music scene. Take a chance. It's way cheaper than the Sunset Strip, and there are no restrictive parking laws.... *Tel 213/413–4442. 1717 Silverlake Blvd., Echo Park. Cover charge.*

The Strip. Huge, multistoried, five host-free bars, and miles of models. It's new and only open one night a week, but when you can drink until you drop, who could manage this more frequently? Live bands, name deejays, and gambling tables for those who are still in touch with their bodies.... *Tel 310/285–8335. 8240 Sunset Blvd., Hollywood. Cover charge.*

Star Strip. All-nude, upscale, big with the tourists.... *Tel 310/652–1741. 365 N. La Cienega Blvd., Los Angeles. Cover charge, one to two drink minimum.*

Star Strip II. The shabbier sibling of the above. Not a great choice for a first date.... *Tel 213/644–1122. 2470 Fletcher Dr., Silverlake. Cover charge, two drink minimum.*

Tiki Ti. A delightful drag night named Club Gloria happens at the otherwise trendoid hangout in Tommy Tang's restaurant. It's not a show so much as an evening with your favorite celluloid dream dates. You go, girl!... *Tel 213/937–5733. 7313 Melrose Ave., Hollywood. Cover charge.*

Troubadour. Phoenixlike, the Troub has risen from the ashes of disastrous booking policies of the eighties, which made bands pay to take the stage. Now it's taking chances again, booking weird and mainstream alike.... *Tel 310/276–6168. 9081 Santa Monica Blvd., West Hollywood. Cover charge.*

Union. Locals love it. It's easy to miss and surrounded by hipper joints, but this tiny bar at the edge of the Strip manages to get by on word of mouth. Let the trendoids waste their money across the street at Roxbury. The best night is Monday for Toledo.... *Tel 213/654–1001. 8210 Sunset Blvd., Hollywood.*

The Viper Room. It used to be a dive, then an in-crowd hangout for name rockers and actors looking for a safe slum of their own. Now it's just over the cusp of one famous overdose and too much bad publicity. The booking policy goes up and down, and when it's up, you'll find it hard to get in. If it's down, then no sweat.... *Tel 310/358–1880. 8852 Sunset Blvd., West Hollywood. Cover charge.*

The West End. A Santa Monica club that feels like a slow neighborhood bar. No cover Mondays; occasional charge Tuesdays to Thursdays.... *Tel 310/394–4647. 1301 5th St., Santa Monica. Cover charge sometimes.*

Whiskey A Go-Go. This is the center of the Sunset Strip's soul, where all those bands of the sixties began, where all those punk bands of the seventies burned out. It's still happening, still a scene. You haven't done the L.A. club scene until you've come to the Whiskey. No age limit. Monday nights are free if you're old enough to drink.... *Tel 310/535–0579. 8901 Sunset Blvd., West Hollywood. Cover charge; no cover Mon.*

Santa Monica Clubs

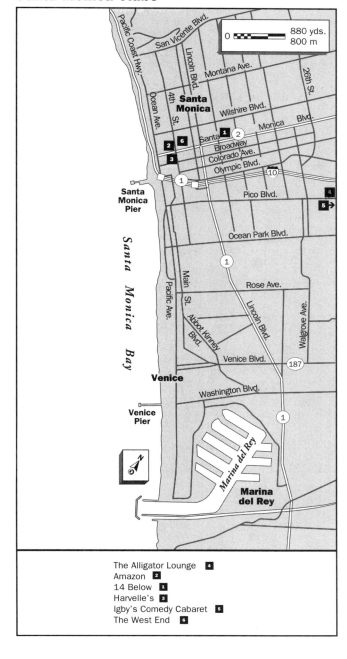

The Alligator Lounge **4**
Amazon **2**
14 Below **1**
Harvelle's **3**
Igby's Comedy Cabaret **5**
The West End **6**

West Hollywood Area Clubs

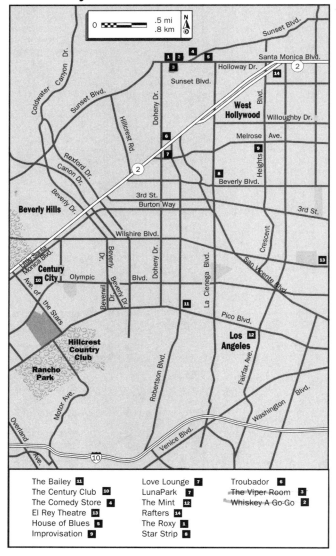

The Bailey **11**
The Century Club **10**
The Comedy Store **4**
El Rey Theatre **13**
House of Blues **5**
Improvisation **9**

Love Lounge **7**
LunaPark **7**
The Mint **12**
Rafters **14**
The Roxy **1**
Star Strip **8**

Troubador **6**
The Viper Room **3**
Whiskey A Go-Go **2**

Hollywood Area Clubs

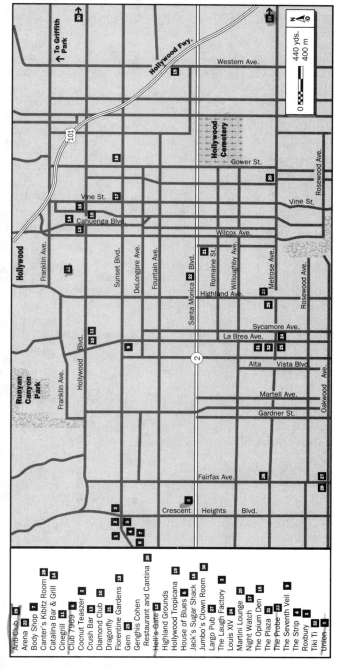

the bar

scene

2

For decades, L.A.'s best
bar scenes existed mainly
on paper, in the gumshoe
world of Raymond
Chandler and Ross
MacDonald. Sure, you
could get a drink easily,

but given the city's conservative heritage, bright talk over strong spirits wasn't a fashionable choice for a night out. There didn't seem to be an L.A. equivalent of the Algonquin, a clubby meeting place for well-known drunks to trade witty barbs.

Well, that's all changed now, thanks in large part to an odd melding of Gen X and grown-up punks, both of whom have learned to appreciate a good, stiff shot in sophisticated surroundings. Twenty years ago, the only hip drinking venues involved live music, art performances, or music-of-the-moment dance scenes. Now bars have come into their own in a generation of places that try to look like sleek hotel bars. The soundtrack is kept low, the martinis are dry, the conversation sparkling. And quite often a salty side dish of irony is provided free next to the peanuts.

That's not a citywide trend. The real thing still exists: piano bars, Tiki bars, pool bars, and, well, bar bars—"dives" we used to call them. The patron saint of such establishments, Charles Bukowski, is no longer with us, and gone are the glorious nights when the bartenders at the Firefly would douse the bar with lighter fluid and, to the bleary delight of comatose drunks, light it on fire. But the spirit(s) live on, fueling a new Los Angeles phenomenon known as Lounge Culture, whereby scary holes-in-the-wall transform overnight into stylish dens packed with industry kids acting like Mickey Rourke in *Barfly* acting like Bukowski. As always in L.A., you can't tell the snake from the tail as it eats itself—but that won't stop you from having a swell time. Lounge Culture is so big here it has its own spin-off soundtrack music, commonly known (and marketed) as *space-age bachelor pad music* (yes, there is an album out—think xylophones meet surf guitars). The whole thing is like Mickey Rooney and Judy Garland putting on a show in the old barn after a dozen martinis.

Los Angeles claims to be the place that spawned bowl-size tropical rum drinks, so it would be silly to come here and not sample them. Drinking can also be a cross-cultural experience of sorts in L.A., courtesy of the large British expat population here. The pub scene is still largely centered in Santa Monica, but there are a few Irish and English pubs servicing dartheads to the east of the 405 freeway, complete with pub food, loud drunks, and football without helmets.

The coffeehouse phenomenon is old news here, but somehow keeps adjusting to the times. Just a few years ago, the mismatched furniture, the various cappuccino and espresso concoctions, and the moody neo-Beat clientele was all you needed. Now coffeehouses offer everything but a hot-wax service for your car: comedy, jazz, poetry, Internet connections, ad hoc theater, computers by the hour, networking sources. Oh, and coffee. And teas. And ginseng. And smart drinks. And the neo-Beats are still there, of course, although not as *en vogue* as they once were.

Drinking Hours

No alcohol can be served after 2am in the state of California. This is the best rule of thumb for figuring out when your favorite establishment closes its doors. Exceptions will be mentioned in the Index, but the only reason most places will close early is you're the last one there and have just gone over your credit limit.

Etiquette

A message on behalf of your waiter or waitress: Yes, they get paychecks, but it's usually not much over minimum wage, and I couldn't survive on it. Could you? I tip between 15 percent and 25 percent of the tab, even if I'm picking up the drink myself directly from the bar. Of course I never use valet parking, so go figure.

User's caveat: Be aware. It's been estimated that on the Hollywood Freeway after the 2am last call on weekends, 30 percent of the drivers are legally drunk. The highway patrol knows this too, and a DWI citation will possibly get your license revoked and set you back about $3,000 after all the legal mea culpas are resolved.

And no, if requested to take a breath test, you can't just drive away. If you're visiting bars in West Hollywood, you might want to look into **The Nightline**, a unique public transportation service offered by the local city fathers. You park at the Pacific Design Center for $2.50 (free with validation at some local businesses) and wait for the bus. It runs every ten minutes in each direction on Santa Monica Boulevard, from San Vicente Boulevard to Fuller Avenue, until 3:30 on the weekends and 2:30 the rest of the week. (See Down and Dirty for more on public transportation.)

The Lowdown

The real thing... In L.A. it seems we tear down our landmarks to make way for minimalls, blowing up that classic Jetsons-style coffeeshop for a strip of fast-food outlets and a liquor store. There are a few of the legends still around, showing up their younger imitators with a style that simply can't be copied. Like the **Tiki Ti** way up Sunset Boulevard in Los Feliz, the archetypal Tiki bar and reportedly the place where many of Trader Vic's tropical fruit juice concoctions originated. Since 1961, this tiny hole-in-the-wall has been an alcoholic E-Ticket everyone has to ride at least once. It's beyond small—only a handful of bar stools and six small tables—but the drinking choices are giant, as long as you like rum. There are 42 different combos, including Skull & Bones, Bonnie & Clyde, and Never-Say-Die. Day-Glo artifacts behind the bar heighten the effects of disorientation, although after one of Ray's Specials (three shots of liquor plus fruit juice) you may not even notice. The bar gets packed on the weekends—not too hard considering the size. Caveat: The drinks go down easily, tasting more of fruit than alcohol, but they pack a massive wallop and you won't know how drunk you are until you try to find your car. Bonus point: You never have to worry about figuring out your bill. All but four of the 72 drink possibilities cost $6.

Another historical landmark is the **Formosa Cafe**, probably the most famous bar in Hollywood for generations of actors, agents, and studio drones. Having survived a recent developer's attempt to demolish it, the red-on-red, shacklike structure—actually a converted railway car—continues to pack in the faithful. The walls are covered with thousands of signed actors' 8-by-10 glossies, many dating back to the forties, everybody from Marilyn Monroe to David Soul. The drinks are killer-strong, the Chinese food killer-lousy, the ambience 100 percent genuine. It's the perfect place to pitch a script, and your mere presence shows you know your Hollywood history. Weekend nights it's jammed with youngsters. Drink anything made with gin or vodka, you won't be disappointed.

And then there's the **Bar Deluxe** in Hollywood. It's not as venerable as either of the above two choices, but is as real as it gets when it comes to Hollywood. There's live music here, but that's not what brings in the regulars. Instead, it's the grimy, gritty, scrape-off-your-shoes feel. Come on a weekday night and compare tattoos.

The faux thing... It's getting so you don't know where to drink anymore. Is that decrepit watering hole on the corner really a dive or just pretending to be one, the result of careful decorating to bring in the free-spending younger clientele who are so enamored of the Bukowski-dive drinking scene of yesteryear? Older drinkers take note: Polish those shoes! If you're 50 and frumpy, your barmates may think you came in here to drink. Especially at the Tiki-redux bars, the most popular style of late: lava lamps, plastic neon artifacts, fake bamboo railings, and a youthful crowd. The best virtual bar of the bunch is **The Lava Lounge** in Hollywood. They have live music, but it's really an afterthought, the stage being so small you might stumble on it on the way to the toilets. Located in the seedy La Brea Sunset Plaza strip mall, it feels like fifties Hollywood. From the street it looks like a local alkies hole, but inside it's soothing and cozy. The trippy blend of surf guitar and jazz (Sinatra to acid) makes total sense. It's generic tropical, "a paradise in the middle of hell" according to owner-booker Michelle. Think *Pulp Fiction* as you ease back into the red roll-and-tuck booths and admire the fake lava walls. Face in the crowd: Quentin Tarantino (naturally). Bonus points: Super friendly bartenders, small covers.

The **Good Luck Club**, in Los Feliz, is another faux dive, its details too perfect to be original, the clientele too young to be serious. More of those comfy, red, roll-and-tuck booths, Chinese lanterns hanging everywhere, bamboo facades, and a small, U-shaped bar that has everything from tropical drinks to your standard mixes and beers. It feels like a hip, local, east-side crowd, interracial and young, but the doorman says many are from the west side, having come over for a cheap drink and no attitude.

It's a good place to pick up someone with brains. It used to be a gay square-dancing club, and if that doesn't work as a trivia pickup line, you need another drink.

Postmodern speakeasies... Don't be surprised if you can't find **3 of Clubs** the first time. Perched at the side of a particularly bombed-out looking minimall on the corner of Santa Monica and Vine, this cozy, refurbished bar has no sign or lights on the sidewalk. The windows are grated over and unless you feel music thumping through the wall, you could easily think you've got the wrong address. The entrance is on Vine, underneath the battered Bargain Clown Mart sign. Once inside it's the decor you'd expect: red on black with a low sparkle ceiling. It's dark and pleasant, the perfect place to enjoy a Scotch (they have 25 to choose from) or a nice microbrew from the tap. There's a side room for live shows (Tuesdays and Thursdays), a deejay on Wednesdays. It feels like a small Vegas lounge, off the Strip, the kind of place where the dealers and pit bosses hang after work. It's crowded on weekends and particularly popular with youngish actors and musicians.

In the same mode is **The Room**, whose door on Cahuenga is always firmly locked. You can hear a party going on, but can't come in unless you walk into the alleyway just east. Look for the bouncer-doorman hanging out near the garbage cans. It's small (50 people would pack it if they could find it) and dark as a pit. Again, there's a healthy selection of single malts. It's a very private clubhouse but without any cliquey in-crowd-only atmosphere. You can get sloppy drunk here, confess secrets, and generally embarrass yourself just in front of your friends.

Slumming... As a new generation discovers the joys of hard liquor, a variety of anonymous dives around town have found a new following. And massive redecorating is not always necessary. Until a few years ago, the **Smog Cutter** was the sort of bar you'd step past briskly, perhaps feeling some pity for the barflies nursing wake-up beers. Well, now you'll just feel envy. The Smog Cutter has been discovered in a big way, and on weekend nights you may not even be able to squeeze in. Unlike other faux dives, this is that unique survivor, maintaining a foot in both generations; slow and measured during the week and then, on

Friday and Saturday nights, it lurches into an intoxicating karaoke-driven swirl. The crowd is youngish, hip, grunge-damaged. Your bartender may be Lynn, a petite Vietnamese woman who runs the bar with the banter of bartenders everywhere. Yet she knows the regulars on non-karaoke nights, pouring their drinks the moment they come in the door.

Pleasantly aged and reeking of character, the **Burgundy Room** on Cahuenga is long and narrow and has only one booth for more laid-back relaxing. But the bar counter is comfortable, the lighting soothingly dim, and the mood casual. It's nowhere near as much of a scene as other places in the neighborhood (like **The Room,** just across the street), but that works in its favor. You won't see any models at the **H.M.S. Bounty,** near Vermont and Wilshire, highlighted by the "Food & Grog" sign above the entrance. There's Glenn Miller on the jukebox, metal portholes (with mirrors instead of glass) scattered around the room, paintings of classic sailing ships, a three-master model behind the bar. There's lots of wood and, with the still-closed Ambassador Hotel across the street, a sense of good days long gone. *L.A. Magazine* called this the "best dive" in the city in 1995. I wouldn't go that far, but those red roll-and-tuck booths are comfortable, the drinks strong, and it's open every night of the year. What more could you ask for?

Droppings on the Rat Pack trail... Dino may be gone, but his spirit lives on at ring-a-ding-ding piano bars like **Bob Burns Restaurant** in Santa Monica. It has Scottish clan emblems and red-and-black tartan carpeting. Sitting on the stools that hug the piano, nursing a Scotch (what else?), you wouldn't be surprised to see Sammy, Joey, and Frank come swaggering in, having just tossed the keys to Kookie to park the 'vette. There are some truly sad drunks here, but hey... that's not you! (Yet.) It's also a restaurant (which is why most people come), but no haggis, no shepherd's pie, no trifle. Get a large Caesar salad and ask for the theme to the Pack classic, *Ocean's Eleven*. Farther east on Wilshire is **Bob Henry's Round Table,** another restaurant-and-piano-bar window on the past. Like Bob Burns, it's strictly a place for your parents to visit seriously, or you with a well-cultured sense of irony. Take a stool at the bar, watch the mirror over the piano player's hands, and request "Lithium" by Nirvana and see how he does. Be a real American—have a slab of prime rib as big as your head. This is the place for it. The more red meat and hard liquor you shovel into your face, the more you'll enjoy yourself. Much farther east is **The Dresden Restaurant and Lounge**, in Los Feliz, right next door to Amok Books (a major source of the most disturbing and scary literature available anywhere, covering cults, bondage, S&M, survivalist tracts, and ultranoir fiction). Amok plus Dresden is a marriage made in hell. Inside the airy Dresden Room, it's all brick and wood, with a surf-and-turf dining room that packs in the seniors on weekends. You get the sense of a Bavarian castle warmed by roaring fire. This is the kind of place David Lynch comes to unwind. At the requisite piano bar off to the side, there's (not surprisingly, given the neighborhood) a large assort-ment of young, vaguely disaffected drinkers, their Amok purchases sensibly wrapped in brown paper. They're not out for an evening of irony. This *is* their local bar. And that in itself is scary enough.

Yuppie pool halls... Remember when pool halls were synonymous with lowlifes and shady deals? Well, it's still true. Only now a valet parks your Lexus while you take a meeting over solids and stripes. The elegant **Hollywood Athletic Club** is undoubtedly the apex of the yup-pool genre locally, and it's easy to see why this is such a popu-lar hangout for industry types. It's absolutely stunning inside, from the brass foot railings to the heavy, carved colonial-style beams. The building dates from 1924 and has been renovated to glorious condition. There are TV monitors scattered around but kept tastefully mute. Beyond the shutters you can see traffic crawling by on Sunset, but in here the only worry is if you're being hus-tled or not. There are 40 tables, excellent lighting, quite respectable California cuisine, and a full bar. This isn't the pool hall on the corner your mother warned you about. Best of all, you don't have to play to have a good time. Just sipping a Chardonnay and watching from one of the stools is an evening's entertainment by itself. They have an excellent pro shop as well. A similar mood (but no valet parking) is found in Santa Monica at **Gotham Hall**, on the Third Street Promenade. It sits on the second floor and boasts tremendously high ceilings, a purple-burgundy color scheme, and a soundtrack that is targeted more for a party than pitching that miniseries. The clientele is west-side yups, their dates, and only a few seriously hungry cue sharks. Extra bonus points for the soft purple hue of the felt. There's a great sound system as well, and if your game is off, the bar overlooks the promenade.

A real pool hall... This is much more like what your mom had in mind when she told you to stop hanging around that corner pool hall. When you approach the door of **Babe Brandelli's Brig** in Venice, you know this is not some west-side facsimile of a dive but the real thing. The sign out front has a Dempsey-like boxer crouched in a pugilist stance, and from the street you hear slurring voices muttering "fuckin' shit..." It's just somebody grousing over their stickwork at the pool table. This is a true locals bar, where tough-looking guys with greasy, long hair drink real drinks, sport truck-stop tattoos (not the modern-primitive type), argue about sports, and play excellent cutthroat pool at three always-busy tables.

Where to meet cops... **The Short Stop** has been around for 25 years, and for a while it was a major Dodgers hangout. Fifteen years ago you could stop in for a beer and see Garvey playing pool, Baker playing pinball. But those days are gone. "They're all drinking Perrier," groused a veteran on a quiet afternoon. Now it's back to being a sports bar for fans only, especially after a game at nearby Dodger Stadium, and a major hangout for LAPD cops coming home from work from the equally nearby Police Academy. Want to talk swings and hits? Come by on payday and mix with the Thin Blue Line.

Where to feel no pressure... Part of the ever-expanding scene in Los Feliz, **Vida** is a welcome addition. The semicircular bar, backed by three round mirrors, is a great setting in which to do your Thin Man impressions. Ask Hector the bartender for a cigarette, and he'll deliver with a flourish from a colorful, wooden Oriental box. The food, contemporary American fare courtesy of Fred Eric, formerly of the industry hangout the Olive, is reasonable in price and tasty. Patrons include everyone from ABC-TV producers (the studios are right around the corner) to punks from Epitaph Records (also right around the corner). Bonus points: They have a nice private room where you can sit on the floor, Japanese style, on tatami mats. Also a low-key bar with a great clientele and friendly staff is **Smalls**, near Paramount on Melrose. No sign out front, but look for the boxing gloves hanging above the front door. It looks like a bar that once lived off the guys who work in the body shop next door, but it's been ever-so-subtly tweaked—large, vintage photos of boxers adorn the walls—so that anyone could come in and feel immediately welcome. They often have live music (although there's no stage per se) and, of course, never a cover. One of the best of the best. Also on Melrose, **The Snakepit** is the ideal neighborhood bar. Even though the wall o' liquor behind the counter suggests this is hard-drinking heaven, most people seem to be sucking down brew. There are 19 beers on tap, nothing more than $3.50. The predominant decor is beer signs, the clientele Melrose retail drones, shoppers, locals, tourists. It's loud, has two large TV screens at either end of the bar (each set to a different sports channel), decent food (although not much room to eat it in), and zero attitude. "I just get mad when people smoke pot in here," the bartender told me, "not when they don't tip." If you're feeling a bit wobbly on your pins, point your nose across the street to the **Java Joint** for a double espresso.

Where to watch sports... Roll back that work shirt and hoist one. You're in the **Tavern on Main**, a few blocks from Venice Beach. They've got 39 beers, but basically you only come here to shout at the TV. Single men belly up to the bar and watch sports intently. It's got a black-marble bar, brass railings, and a sports-bar feel. Want to cry in your beer? Come here. Or for a slightly more downscale experience, stumble across the street to the **Circle Bar**. It should be called the Oval Bar since that's the shape of the bar in the center of this one-room joint, but I doubt any of the patrons quibble about it. The art on the walls looks like the sort of thing you buy by the pound at a garage sale, and pretty much sets the tone. This is a locals bar, where you come to drink, play some pool, get drunk, maybe get into a fight, maybe pick up a warm body to take home. Nearby there's the **Oar House**, decorated with a bizarre assortment of artifacts: saddles, bits and halters, a stagecoach, and pair of horses tilted sideways, frozen in motion sideways on the ceiling. Locals come to the Oar House, but there are also those wandering in just to grab a handful of free peanuts from the big barrel in back. There's sawdust on the floor, an electronic dartboard, and a sound system that would do a dance hall proud. But obviously there's a potentially nasty edge here—everything comes served in plastic glasses. If you're looking for a TV on Melrose, try the homey **Snakepit**. Near Dodger Stadium, there's **The Short Stop**.

Where to meet actors... Not every actor with paid-up SAG dues has to be in a trailer at 5am, ready for makeup. Some are actually in between projects. And so they come to **Sanctuary** in Beverly Hills. It's large enough for catty gossiping *entre nous*, yet designed to encourage "the lost art of conversation," according to owner Dimitri Cristoforidis. It's a classical space, dating from the thirties, but the decor—a weird marriage of Frank Lloyd Wright with Francis Bacon—is just a wee bit over-the-top. Of course "Baywatch" babe Pamela Lee *is* a part owner. Be warned—go shopping for a new outfit before you come. A similar snooty mood is found at the **Bar Marmont**, the supposedly "private" adjunct to the famous hotel on Sunset. Behind the funky gate lies a very pleasant two-level space, highlighted by a ceiling plastered with the bodies of thousands of moths (or are they butterflies?). They claim to only admit guests of the hotel, but don't believe it—the famous are always welcome here. What the Marmont strives for and utterly misses—class—you can find at **Jones**. It's elegant without being exclusive, trendy but not trendoid. This is a bar of the moment, managing to blend the famous and the faceless in a cozy space that encourages attitude-free mixing. Egalitarian L.A. at its best, you can park your own car without any sense of shame.

Where to drink mystery punches... In Los Feliz, **Vida** bartender Hector is responsible for dreaming up the daily Road Kill drink special (usually freshly squeezed juice mixed with spicy vodka). As the alleged fountainhead of tropical rum drinks, the **Tiki Ti** is a must-see. After just one of their high-powered mixtures, you won't know what you're drinking. Only that it tastes good and makes you feel better. Then there's always the faux tropical pit stop **The Lava Lounge**.

Where to have a quiet drink... The Sunset Strip is known for over-the-top excess and nonstop, staged media events. But at the understated **Union**, on the east end of the Strip, the mood is low and steady, despite the surrounding frenetic activity of the **Body Shop**, **Roxbury**, and the **Coconut Teaszer** (see The Club Scene), all within spitting distance. That's why it feels so nice here: calm, an island of quiet sanity, *civilized*. And in this era of bunker bars, it has real windows that look out on Sunset, curtains, and a wall of books that swings open to the back patio area. It's small and offers occasional free cabaret-style acts, but there's no actual stage. What you get is a sense of much-needed normalcy.

Martini madness... Yeah, martinis are the drink du jour now, and you'll be able to find great shaken or stirred at **Jones** and **The Room**, but for ambience and history, you can't beat **Musso & Frank's** in Hollywood. This has been a film industry hangout for generations. The food sucks, the waiters are brusque and rude, but the long oak bar was where Raymond Chandler and scores of script-writing hacks drowned their sorrows in search of a story line. It's a local landmark, so at least come by for a drink.

Margarita madness... Many Mexicans believe that drinking tequila before a meal aids indigestion. I don't know about that, but it certainly makes your dining partners more attractive. You can get good margaritas in just about any decent bar, but the quickest route to agave nirvana is sucking them down by the pitcher. Which is why just about everybody I know goes to **El Coyote**. They certainly don't come for the food. The margaritas aren't especially strong, but when you're drinking by the pitcher that's actually a plus. The restaurant is an institution, unfortunately, a place where too many Angelenos got their first taste of what is supposed to be Mexican food. The grub at **El Adobe**, across the street from the Paramount lot, is better, but again it's the margarita pitchers you come for. That and the chance of maybe seeing former governor Jerry Brown stop by—he used to hang here regularly and there's still a large poster of him in the window. One last tip: If you're ordering margaritas, the quality of the tequila is not a factor. Don't waste expensive *anejo* (aged) or *reposado* (rested) tequilas in a mixed drink. The high-quality, 100 percent agave tequilas are best when treated like a single malt whiskey or cognac.

So much beer, so little time... The two most popular beers at **The Brewhouse** on the Third Street Promenade in Santa Monica are Lobotomy Boch, a hefty 12 percent dark, and Raspberry Honeywheat, a fruity, vaguely sweet ale that goes down as easily as the best Czech pilsner. Five 250-gallon beer vats dominate the scene at this surprisingly large brew pub—there are two additional seating areas beyond the front room—and the seats of choice are those at the bar. There are 10 house brews, 13 "guest" beers on tap, and another 10 in bottles. There's also wine and hard cider available, but why bother? The Irish manager, John Harte, designed the menu, and his worldwide wanderings as an itinerant chef come through strong, complementing whatever is in your pint. There's goulash, stuffed jalapeños, pastas, soups, Cajun chicken, and bratwurst—all worth trying. Nothing is over $10. Bonus point: They brew their own, unlike many other micro outlets. The clientele is local, tourist, male, female—just about anyone who appreciates a great beer at a good price. Bigger and more date friendly is the **Library Ale House**, just a short drive south. While the Brewhouse gets a nod for its home-brewed freshness, the Ale House can't be beat for its decor. The interior has four different tropical woods (all from eco-forest reserves). The sign behind the bar—"When brewing is outlawed only outlaws will brew beer"—says it all. Beer is a basic human right. Locals are the main clientele. There are shoji-style lamps, a collection of beer bottles from around the world above the bar, and they take all credit cards "but Chevron and Nordstrom." The kitchen closes at 11:30, but before then it serves standard American cuisine, supplemented by mango salsas and a few vegetarian selections. It's pedestrian friendly, community oriented, and the resident beer expert is a woman. It's also crowded on the weekends, which may send you to the outside patio where the smokers congregate underneath ficus trees. If you come often enough, get a Library Card: after imbibing 27 of their beers, you get a free T-shirt—and after 27 brews, you'd better ask for an X-Large. Almost the opposite in character is **Father's Office** on Montana. The long, narrow room with a bar at the end feels more like a coffeehouse than a microbrew outlet. The tables and chairs are beat up and anonymous. They don't do any in-house brewing but do have a hefty selection (31 at last count). You won't see any would-be screenwriters worrying over their laptops here. Instead, this is the kind of place where you can sink into your own funk or have a very intense conversation with your date.

LOS ANGELES **⚭ THE BAR SCENE**

Rooms with views... For sheer visual splendor, it's hard to beat **Windows on Hollywood**, the revolving circular bar perched on the 23rd floor of the Holiday Inn on Highland. Sure you have to walk through the lobby to get to it, but once you're seated it's suddenly 1972 again and the future looks bright. Knock back a few and watch the world spin while cheesy cabaret acts (also circa 1972) vie for your attention. This is high on the trendoid hit list. Lower down, but with a more outdoor feel, there's **Yamashiro**, in the hills just above Hollywood Boulevard. The style is some gazpacho blend of Orientalia—Chinese and Japanese—with a nice interior space and a pleasant little garden just a stumble down the hill across the driveway. The drinks are strong, the food lousy, and the view about what you'd get from an LAPD helicopter. The only time locals come here is when they're bringing someone from out of town. It's *that* kind of place.

For a taste of the U.K.... Even though it's miles from Santa Monica, where so much of L.A.'s transplanted British culture is centered, Hollywood's **Cat & Fiddle Pub and Restaurant** should satisfy any Anglophile. There are three indoor rooms softly lit with Tiffany lamps, dartboards, and, in deference to this being Southern California, a large tree-shaded patio with a cooling fountain in the center. The menu here is above the standard pub grub: gravlax, sherry trifle, Scotch eggs, fruit crumbles. Certainly there are other places to get a black and tan in Hollywood, but the relaxed mood here makes this a pub for all seasons. Located close to scores of recording studios, the Cat & Fiddle is a popular hangout for rockers taking a break from session work. Bonus point: live music in the patio. Out in Santa Monica is the mother of all L.A. pubs, **Ye Olde King's Head**. You can't go wrong here, and you can't hear yourself think. Which is why you came in the first place. It's loud, noisy, and Creedence Clearwater is blasting on the sound system. The action at the dartboards is frantic and serious, while somewhere in one of the quieter back rooms, a family is dining on crispy fish and chips, liberally seasoned with the tasty vinegar that sits on every table. The place has been popular since the seventies, when a manic piano-playing MC would taunt patrons into drinking contests. You won't see anyone downing a pitcher in one gulp anymore but the place is still a must-visit—like the Pacific Ocean, it's a local landmark. Plus, they have cider on tap. Farther east, **O'Brien's Irish Pub & Restaurant** is way less boisterous. The mood is calmer, more *mature*, if you will, chatty, and convivial. And the food, usually not an attraction at a pub, is excellent, from the Spud Murphy Soup or the corned beef and cabbage, to the Black and White Pudding. Meanwhile, there isn't a tie in sight at **The Bailey**, just south of Beverly Hills. It's a haven for younger Brits and Celts who don't want to make the drive to Santa Monica for that taste of home. It doesn't really feel like a pub, with the fake flower bouquets on the wall, the floor-to-ceiling mirrors, and loud thumping disco-techno pumping out of the sound system. It gets thronged on the weekends. Maybe they've come for the killer Irish coffee.

A sign on the wall of **Molly Malone's** on Fairfax says it's only 40 miles to Dublin, and after a few pints here you might believe it. This is a working-class pub, tough and honest, full of smoke and loud chatter. Standard pub grub is served, but only at lunchtime. A series of truly bad paintings adorns the walls, but nobody seems to care. They have live music every night of the week, often traditionally Irish in style. They're totally jammed on the weekends. Bonus points: At the door, you can pick up a free copy of the *Irish Times.*

Where to take a meeting... You could easily bring your producer to the **Library Ale House** to discuss your treatment, or your lover to discuss your fear of commitment. On Whilshire Boulevard, **O'Brien's** is a businessman's pub filled with Century City nine-to-fivers, both sexes sometimes wearing ties, though only the men have cigars tucked into their white shirt pockets. You will probably hear cultivated accents here, and you may not get a table. Even if you don't know how to play pool, the **Hollywood Athletic Club** has lots of industry movers and shakers, good food, excellent drinks, and even valet parking.

The digital underground... For those who are Net literate, the latest word is always available on-line. You can find out who's where and when (as if you really care), settle that silly sports trivia question, or chat with a bunch of faceless strangers in far-off places while ignoring the physical presence of people around you—all from the "comfort" of a lumpy thrift-store sofa in a coffeehouse in L.A. CafeNet, an L.A.-based computer network, is the medium, and the fast (yet pricey) terminals in coffeehouses around the city are the delivery vehicle. It's something else to do now that gong-show cabaret has invaded the coffeehouse scene. (Maybe virtual reality *is* better than the real thing.) **The Equator Coffee House** in Pasadena's Old Town, and Hollywood's quintessential slacker coffeehouse, **Grounds Zero**, are two jumping off points for CafeNet (at 25¢ per quarter-hour). Though it's in a building dating from the last century, the mood inside Equator is sterile—fitting for Pasadena. Then, out in Venice, there's **Cyber Java**, where Pentium-based workstations, fast T-1 connections, cameras, and teleconferencing software combine to provide a sense of what the Net could be (if only you could afford the memory at home). What does a nerd's New Year's party sound like? Come here and you'll get an idea (plus a very decent double espresso). On-line time is not cheap—$7.50 an hour—but far more entertaining than watching Jean-Claude Stallonegger attempt a new facial expression. This is as close as you can get to what the hype promises. Up the street, at the **World Cafe**, it's the first mixture of on-line high jinks with real-time alcohol. It seems like a natural. Everyone knows the clock ticks more quickly when you can't read the dial—especially if you're trying to type at the same time. Located on the lip of the upscale strip of Santa Monica's Main Street, the World sits back from the sidewalk and has a nice foliage-filled patio, an underwater motif in the main dining room, and even a dance area where jazz, blues, and R&B try to compete with the cathode-screen jive.

Just over the hills from Hollywood in the Cahuenga pass is **Industry Cyber-Cafe**, probably the most essential coffeehouse in L.A. for would-be actors, screenwriters, producers, directors, and others trying to break into the entertainment business. It has computers for rent, screenwriting software, a mailbox drop, résumé services, acting and writing workshops, on-line connections, and, by the way, coffees and teas. It is, as promised, "the ultimate entertainment-industry resource center." Open until 2 on weekends, midnight the rest of the week.

Best unintentional self-parody... Milk Bar is just the sort of place you'd think a former Studio 54 bartender would bring to Beverly Hills. No bar stools, but a lot of the clientele probably don't have enough butt-cheek cellulite left to make true barfly perching a possibility. Here they lounge and slump, imagining themselves acting out scenes from *Less Than Zero*. It's named after a defunct New York establishment, and like the pale imitation it is, fails to satisfy unless it's the first time Mom let you have the Porsche and you're really, really excited. Like something out of an old SCTV skit—but without the writing.

Hotel bars... People in L.A. don't really relate to the concept of spending time in a hotel lounge unless you're actually staying there. After all, if you had a car to get across town, wouldn't you? Well, here are a few places that transcend that generic stigma. West Hollywood's **Mondrian Hotel Lounge** is a study in black on black, with walls, tables, and the soft furniture all done in variations of ebony. And there's a nice, black baby grand piano, expertly manipulated by a musician (all in black, natch) who plays off-kilter standards with true hotel panache. This is a popular hangout for touring bands who are playing the Sunset Strip, so it offers a very interesting mix. Plus, you probably won't have to wait to use the bathroom like you would at the nearby **House of Blues** (see The Club Scene). Far more special in tone is the **Hana Lounge** at the Hotel Nikko in Beverly Hills. The Japanese obviously understand what a good hotel lounge should be—soothing, sophisticated, and a compelling reason not to leave the hotel. There's a pool laid out like a rock garden (although you'll never think you're in Kyoto), comfy leather chairs, and a swing band (Thursdays through Saturdays) that gives you a reason to order yet another drink and maybe a side order of sushi.

The caffeine scene... In L.A., more than in most cities, coffeehouses reflect the neighborhoods. A good example is **Grounds Zero**, hidden inside the courtyard of the Virgin Megastore in Hollywood. Perched at the start of the Sunset Strip, it has a sense of being a Hollywood crossroads, merging weirdos, rock-star wanna-bes, tourists, poets, music- and film-industry drones. In other words, the typical Hollywood gumbo. The sitting area outside is public enough to be unthreatening to the outsider, yet with enough inborn attitude (thanks to the patrons) to be hip.

Open mike night is Mondays, poetry readings are on Wednesdays, art exhibits are held the second Monday of the month. If the readings put you to sleep, try a Richter Scale (a shot of espresso dropped in a cup of French roast) or a Coke-A-Mocha (shots of espresso, Coca-Cola, and chocolate, served over ice). Hours are flexible, but it's often open until 1am on weeknights.

At the opposite end of the spectrum (and town) is **Anastasia's Asylum**, in a nondescript section of Santa Monica. Compared to the retail ambience around it, Anastasia's does seem like a retreat, a place to stop on the way to something else. Long and narrow, there are not a lot of places to sit, but people do like to hang here for a while—paying their bills, dissecting relationships, working on schoolwork. There are tables out front where the smokers sit, surveying the empty sidewalks on Wilshire Boulevard. Inside, the decor is standard schizoid thrift store: comfortable and used. The menu claims the place is "open later than you're awake"—which means until 3 on weekends, 1 during the week. But it's not necessarily the hours that will bring you in; it's the vegetarian menu, a full assortment of dinners, sandwiches, and breakfasts.

There's nothing so elaborate in terms of cuisine (or drinks) at Hollywood's aptly named **Bourgeois Pig**, one of the original first-wave L.A. coffeehouses. Among the archetypes that set the mold for scores of latter-day wanna-beaneries, it's cozy, cool, and dark, dude. *Way* dark. If you buy something to read at the bookstore next door, don't plan on reading it in here. The attraction here is the comfy, mismatched (natch) sofas and chairs scattered around the long, narrow room. That and killer coffees, Italian ices, teas, and bottled fruit drinks. There are two pool tables in the back for those who forgot their laptops and have to do *something* with their hands. Quiet, snug, and open until about 1:30.

Offering a mix of experiences, from board games to rummaging through some fabulous vintage clothes and jewelry, the **All-Star Theatre Cafe & Speakeasy** calls itself "The Ultimate 1920s Coffeehouse." It's certainly the ultimate something, but is it a coffeehouse, a cafe, a speakeasy, or simply the biggest closet you've ever gotten lost in? The espresso won't win any awards, but the wardrobe certainly will (and probably did in various forties films). You feel like you're fingering history when you sort through the beaded evening gowns, fur hats and gloves, buckled shoes, massive costume jewelry. It's for sale—try it on. In Little Tokyo, on the site of the former punk after-hours hangout Atomic Cafe, **Impala** carries on the tradition, staying open until midnight every night but Sunday and offering performances by musicians way above standard coffeehouse-circuit quality. The menu consists of the expected espressos and lattes, as well as a very respectable selection of teas.

If it's too late for coffee, how about a Ginsing Slurpee? In the heart of Pasadena's Old Town, down a narrow walking street, you'll find **The Equator Coffee House**, which has everything from your standard espresso mixtures to protein drinks and a hip new sweet tea beverage mixed with milk and cinnamon, known as Oregon Chai. It's airy and has brick walls, remnants from the building's former life as a stable at the turn of the century. The clientele ranges from Art Center enfants terribles to tourists looking for a quiet haven from the frenetic activity out on Colorado Boulevard. Need to pull an all-nighter? Try a Cardiac Attack (two shots of espresso, banana, fruit juice, and protein powder).

The Index

El Adobe. The food is marginal at best, but the pitchers of margaritas are the best legal high in town. A great party place, as long as there's nobody in the group who expects high cuisine.... *Tel 213/462–9421. 5536 Melrose Ave., Hollywood.*

All-Star Theatre Cafe & Speakeasy. Part vintage clothing store, part coffeehouse, but mainly an aged spinster aunt's cluttered closet, this quirky little adjunct to the historic Hollywood Knickerbocker hotel has to be the oddest java joint in L.A. Open until 3, you could easily spend the entire night in here.... *Tel 213/962–8898. 1714 N. Ivar Ave., Hollywood.*

Anastasia's Asylum. In a bland section of Santa Monica, this is an asylum—especially if it's late. Anastasia's is open until 3 on the weekends, 1 on Sundays, and 2 the rest of the week. Unlike most late-night coffeehouses, they have a very large and complete menu, nearly entirely vegetarian, from lasagna to steamed egg dishes.... *Tel 310/394–7113. 1028 Wilshire Blvd., Santa Monica.*

Babe Brandelli's Brig. You want a real bar? No yuppies, no grunge revivalists, or buzz-cut wanna-bes? Come here. This is the real thing with hard-ass drinkers, hard-ass pool players, hard-ass babes hanging at the bar.... *No telephone. Abbot Kinney Blvd. near Venice Blvd., Venice.*

The Bailey. High ceilings, a long bar framed by a huge mirror, and Art Deco couches, this is an odd mix of pub and generic dance club. It's a major home away from home for young British expats. Great beers, excellent sound, a tiny dance floor, and a cozy schmooze room in the back make it a good place to find a new friend.... *Tel 310/275–2619. 8771 W. Pico Blvd. (at Robertson), Los Angeles.*

Bar Deluxe. Even though it's newly renovated, this is still down and dirty Hollywood. It's kept real dark here (probably with good reason), and the bruiser at the door isn't checking you for your clothes, but for any sociopathic attitude that might create problems. You want to really see what Hollywood is like? Come here for a beer. If there's music, you won't be disappointed—especially if you drink enough.... *Tel 213/ 469–1991. 1710 N. Las Palmas Ave., Hollywood.*

Bar Marmont. It tries to be an ultrachic, private hangout for the glitterati. Just say you're staying at the hotel or that you're a producer meeting with some agents and you'll get in. The drinks are overpriced, but it's worth a visit just to check out their lepidopteran collection on the ceiling.... *Tel 213/650–0575. 8171 Sunset Blvd., Hollywood.*

Bob Burns Restaurant. Soft leather seats, wood walls, Scottish memorabilia, and a piano-bar mood that will transport you back to 1955. The menu never seems to change, the patrons are rooted to their bar stools; the only thing moving is the flickering flame of the gas lamps.... *Tel 310/ 393–6777. 202 Wilshire Blvd., Santa Monica.*

Bob Henry's Round Table. Another piano bar–restaurant frozen in time, the Round Table is full of character and provokes either wonderful sentimentality or raging depression. Depends on how many drinks you've had, maybe. Red-and-black vinyl, heavy wooden beams, a certain Teutonic heaviness that settles on everything. If it's full, check out Bob Burns.... *Tel 310/828–2217. 2460 Wilshire Blvd., Santa Monica.*

Bourgeois Pig. Too dark, kind of cluttered and barlike, the Pig is one of the originals in the coffeehouse wars.... *Tel 213/ 962–6366. 5931 Franklin Ave., Hollywood.*

The Brewhouse. Ignore the location. If this was down in Venice, off a crack alley, it would be the hangout of all sorts of celebs. Right now it's mecca for micro addicts. They have the best home-brewed beer in L.A. After two glasses you'll forget you're on the Promenade.... *Tel 310/393–2629. 1246 Third Street Promenade, Santa Monica.*

Burgundy Room. It's a dive—small, dark, and Hollywood friendly. Ten years ago you wouldn't have been caught dead here, but now it's a trendy place to take a *very* low-key meeting.... *Tel 213/465–7530. 1621½ Cahuenga Blvd., Hollywood.*

Cat & Fiddle Pub and Restaurant. Hollywood's best-known pub cleanly blends a California outdoors feel with the coziness of a traditional public house. The food is more than decent, the beers reasonable and varied. Who comes? Industry insiders, journalists, soccer lovers, Scotch-egg addicts.... *Tel 213/468–3800. 6530 Sunset Blvd., Hollywood.*

Circle Bar. Want to see what Main Street was like before it was gentrified? Step into this one-room bar and talk to some of the locals and see what they think. It has zero attitude and a working-class feel—the perfect antidote to the *très chic* ambience everywhere else in the neighborhood.... *Tel 310/ 392–4898. 2926 Main St., Santa Monica.*

El Coyote. This is a place to drink margaritas, not eat Mexican food. If you must have something solid before you order that next pitcher, go for something really safe, chips and guacamole. The food is way terrible.... *Tel 213/939–2255. 7312 Beverly Blvd., Los Angeles.*

Cyber Java. This small Venice coffeehouse is as good as it gets for L.A.'s caffeine-addled Internet surfers. It has a convivial atmosphere even though people are staring at terminals more intently than they do at each other. Superfast connections, adequate coffee.... *Tel 310/581–1300. 1029 Abbot Kinney Blvd., Venice.*

The Dresden Restaurant and Lounge. You won't find anything cozier than this. The neighborhood is way cool, goatee friendly, and presents a ready mind meld with Frank and Sammy, circa 1962. A piano bar in the middle of a dying culture.... *Tel 213/665–4294. 1760 N. Vermont Ave. (at Hollywood), Los Feliz.*

The Equator Coffee House. It feels old but has been retrofitted with cyber equipment. This haven from the traffic on Old Town's streets is quiet yet impersonal. At least there's an Internet box so you won't feel lonely. Has CafeNet terminal.... *Tel 818/564–8656. 22 Mills Place (at Colorado), Pasadena.*

Father's Office. No decor really, worn wooden tables, and the general feel of beer lover's clubhouse, with 31 micro variations available. A good place to come and have a quiet chat with a friend.... *Tel 310/451–9330. 1018 Montana Ave., Santa Monica.*

Formosa Cafe. This is one of the handful of genuine L.A. Tiki bar/Chinese restaurants that are now being copied by every former dive in town. A landmark that must be visited. Still popular with filmland veterans, journalists, and L.A. natives, it's recently been discovered by the Lounge Culture set.... *Tel 213/850–9050. 7156 Santa Monica Blvd., Hollywood.*

Good Luck Club. Chinese-tropical decor, a trendy east-side crowd mixed with slumming 20-to-30-somethings from west of La Brea. Loud, chatty, and friendly, it feels like a secret bar from the fifties, despite the crush of beautiful young people.... *Tel 213/666–3524. 1514 Hillhurst Ave., Los Feliz.*

Gotham Hall. As the name suggests, this pool hall and bar mixture doesn't take itself too seriously. Wonderful purple felt on the tables, high ceilings, and a very elegant bar from which you can either watch the stickwork at the tables or the human zoo out on the Promenade.... *Tel 310/394–8865. 1431 Third Street Promenade, Santa Monica.*

Grounds Zero. Right at the start of the Sunset Strip, across the street from the Coconut Teaszer, this is the perfect Hollywood coffeehouse, offering poetry readings, high-powered joe, gourmet desserts, and a casual place to hang until way late (midnight or 1 on weekdays, 2 on weekends). CafeNet terminal. The fact that the Virgin Megastore is right next door is an added bonus.... *Tel 213/874–2261. 7554 Sunset Blvd., Hollywood.*

Hana Lounge. This is what every hotel lounge should be like, something old, something new, something totally ancient. The chairs are American in comfort, while the decor is Japanese in simplicity and elegance.... *Tel 310/247–0400. In the Nikko Hotel, 465 S. La Cienega Blvd., Beverly Hills.*

H.M.S. Bounty. Dive! Dive! Dive! You could get deeper than this but hardly more real. As popular with the elderly denizens of the low-rise apartment-hotels in the neighborhood as with their slightly younger peers, still employed in nearby Wilshire Boulevard offices. You've been warned.... *Tel 213/ 385–7275. 3357 Wilshire Blvd., Los Angeles.*

Hollywood Athletic Club. Wonderfully restored to its twenties grandeur, this is as much a *muy elegante* pool hall (with 40 well-maintained tables) as a place to take a meeting. This is a landmark of SoCal hacienda architecture and is worth a visit even if you don't know which end of the stick to chalk.... *Tel 213/962–6600. 6525 Sunset Blvd., Hollywood.*

Impala. This fairly new coffeehouse offers the usual caffeinated brews, an impressive range of teas, and quality musical performances, staying open until the witching hour (except on Sunday nights). It's not quite the Jabberjaw of Little Tokyo, but they're working up to it.... *Tel 213/621–2170. 418 E. First St., Little Tokyo.*

Industry Cyber-Cafe. This is the ultimate coffeehouse for struggling actors, screenwriters, or anybody trying to break into the Industry. Besides great coffee they have résumé services, scripts and how-to books, writing and acting workshops, a mailbox service, and computers for rent. An essential resource center that is totally unique.... *Tel 213/845– 9998. 3191 Cahuenga Blvd. W, West Hollywood.*

Java Joint. For such a trendoid section of Melrose you'd expect a better coffeehouse than this. It's open until 1 on the weekends, midnight the rest of the week, but the only reason to stop in is because it's convenient to your crosstown drive. Or else you've just stumbled out of The Snakepit and need an eye-opener. Standard mismatched sofas and chairs, three rows of unread books.... *Tel 213/951–0782. 7420½ Melrose Ave., Hollywood.*

Jones. An elegant yet comfortable bar, set up for major gabfests. It has the feel of a Manhattan private club, with large black-and-white photos of L.A. on the walls and what looks like a decade's worth of whiskey bottles stacked behind chicken wire above the counter. Very popular with the industry, musicians, and common folk.... *Tel 213/850–1727. 7205 Santa Monica Blvd., Hollywood.*

The Lava Lounge. For such a small place you'd never expect such a giant buzz. Surf-guitar music, brain-killing tropical drinks, comfy booths, and a Vegas-style sign out front. Minuscule covers and a *très* hip clientele.... *Tel 213/876–6612. 1533 N. La Brea Ave., Hollywood.*

Library Ale House. Need to do some research on your History of Hops thesis? No books to check out but lots of beers— 27 at last count, all of them West Coast microbrews. And if you're not sure what to order, ask for a free taste in a shot glass. Good food offered as well, and a very pleasant outdoor patio in back.... *Tel 310/314–4855. 2911 Main St., Santa Monica.*

Milk Bar. How much UV-lit Plexiglas can you take? It'll take more than exists to make this Bev Hills absurdity a contender. Still, if you like mixing with a crowd of pimply hipsters who think "Melrose Place" is a documentary, come on down! Retro-Bowie and pretend cocktail dresses are okay. Decent drinks, better food.... *Tel 310/276–6355. 453 N. Canon Dr., Beverly Hills.*

Molly Malone's. This is the best blend of pub and underground-music club you'll find in L.A. It may be traditional Irish tunes or something more electrified. Whatever it is, the crowd is genial, young, underdressed, and a mix of Brits and Angelenos. The club itself won't win any awards for decor but who cares?... *Tel 213/935–1577. 575 S. Fairfax Ave., Fairfax.*

Mondrian Hotel Lounge. It's a hotel, sure, but somehow it manages to be something a bit more than just a transitory walk-through. Meeting later for a show on the Strip? Come here first for a drink and some sophisticated piano-bar tunes.... *Tel 213/650–8999. 8440 Sunset Blvd., West Hollywood.*

Musso & Frank's. A little slice of movieland history, this Hollywood restaurant has been the hang for screenwriters, producers, and development drones for generations. The food is overcooked, overpriced, and bland, but the martinis are killer.... *Tel. 213/467–5123. 6667 Hollywood Blvd., Hollywood.*

Oar House. Mainly a sports bar, this Santa Monica landmark is a place to slowly sip a beer and wonder why your life isn't better than it is. The decor will blow your mind.... *Tel 310/396–4725. 2941 Main St., Santa Monica.*

O'Brien's Irish Pub & Restaurant. More a restaurant than a pub, this is a place for after-the-trade-show get-togethers. You can make a date or sell the line, depending on your primal urges. At least you'll have a great meal, and the beers provide a pub-verité feel.... *Tel 310/829–5303. 2226 Wilshire Blvd., Santa Monica.*

The Room. Small, dark, and nearly impossible to find, this secret cubbyhole in Hollywood features fine Scotches (liberally dispensed) and just about total privacy. You can't get any more intimate than this in public. The sound is kept to dinner party levels, and martinis are served in chilled glasses. Popular with writers and youngish hipsters. Enter through the alley.... *Tel 213/462–7196. 1626 N. Cahuenga Blvd., Hollywood.*

Sanctuary. A famous-face hot spot, be prepared to melt your plastic if you're going to eat anything substantial. The mood is European, the decor a bizarre blend of Gaudí and Frank Lloyd Wright. Dress like you can afford the place.... *Tel 310/358–0303. 180 N. Robertson Blvd., Beverly Hills.*

The Short Stop. The place where you're least likely to get mugged in the parking lot has to be this three-room bar a baton's swing from Dodger Stadium and the LAPD training academy. This is a major hangout for off-duty cops so don't ask if they've got Ice-T on the jukebox. Friendliest night: Payday.... *Tel 213/250–5902. 1444 Sunset Blvd., Echo Park.*

Smalls. It's been through the trendoid mill and managed to stay real. With a body shop next door and no name out front, it's only slightly difficult to find and the spartan tone makes it a low-attitude, secret pleasure. Occasional live music and always an interesting crowd, this is a perennial favorite.... *Tel 213/469–8258. 5574 Melrose Ave., Hollywood.*

Smog Cutter. Curious about dive culture? Here's the best place to begin your research. It's small, decorated with travel posters, and the bartender has your drink poured before you even sit down. On weekends it's a Gen X karaoke hot spot. Like jazz, you won't understand it until you see it live. And God help you then…. *Tel 213/667–9832. 864 N. Virgil Ave. (at Normal), East Hollywood.*

The Snakepit. Don't be intimidated by the name. This is basically a locals bar, probably the best along this strip of Melrose, where you can relax from too much shopping or complain about that crummy audition. Friendly, loud, fun…. *Tel 213/852–9390. 7529 Melrose Ave., Hollywood.*

Tavern on Main. This is the perfect beach sports bar, with a massive beer list, nonstop games on the TVs, and brass railings. A great place to make a gentleman's bet on the point spread…. *Tel 310/392–2772. 2907 Main St., Santa Monica.*

3 of Clubs. This is a wonderful hideaway. You'll struggle to find the front door—there's no sign out front—but once you do you've reached a bit of heaven. Large enough to wander, cozy enough to feel secure. Plus there's occasional live music and never a cover. Great single-malt selection…. *Tel 213/462–6441. 1122 N. Vine St., Hollywood.*

Tiki Ti. You'll never find a more authentic version of the badly-lit, faux Polynesian, strong-drink nirvana than this L.A. original, in business for 35 years. Clientele is everyone: tourists, locals, dates, rum-lovers. Psychedelic, small, and intoxicating…. *Tel 213/669–9381. 4427 Sunset Blvd., Los Feliz. Open Wed–Sat. No credit cards.*

Union. It's easy to slip past this tiny bar at the edge of the Strip but worth searching out…. *Tel 213/654–1001. 8210 Sunset Blvd., Hollywood.*

Vida. The food here is fabulous, but the bar is even better. It's small and cozy, but somehow you feel you could have a *very* private conversation and Hector, the bartender, wouldn't hear a thing…. *Tel 213/660–4446. 1930 Hillhurst Ave., Los Feliz.*

LOS ANGELES ♩ THE BAR SCENE

Windows on Hollywood. Although the building was redone recently, this revolving bar on the top of the Holiday Inn didn't lose its seventies ambience. It's a trendy hangout for those who consider kitsch a main meal. On the weekends there are probably more goateed and tattooed locals than visiting hotel guests.... *Tel 213/462–7181. 1755 N. Highland Ave., Hollywood.*

World Cafe. In the patio area of this Main Street restaurant/bar, you can touch base with idiots around the world via the Internet. Unlike you, however, they aren't slowly getting drunk on a World Cafe Hula (pineapple, rum, cranberry, and lime) while your spinach pancakes congeal into a soggy mess. Open until 1 on the weekends, with live music in the cafe proper, it's way better than Net-surfing in some musty coffeehouse with a bunch of sober losers.... *Tel 310/392–1661. 2820 Main St., Santa Monica.*

Yamashiro. A weird schizoid-Japanese decor, mediocre food, and slightly overpriced drinks, the only reason you come here is for the view—which can't be beat. People come here for office parties or to show their visiting relatives the sparkling lights of Hollywood. Everyone should come at least once.... *Tel 213/466–5125. 1999 N. Sycamore Ave., Hollywood.*

Ye Olde King's Head. The mother of all L.A. pubs, this Santa Monica landmark is raucous, rambling, intoxicating (in every sense of the word), and the perfect place to bring a date you don't want to talk to. Conversations are shouted, especially around the bar near the dartboards. Lots of fun and better-than-average pub food.... *Tel 310/451–1402. 116 Santa Monica Blvd., Santa Monica.*

Santa Monica Bars

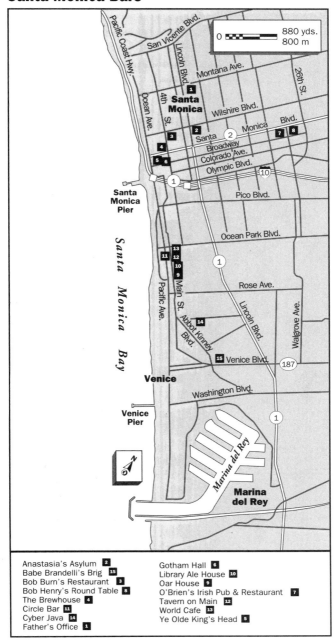

Anastasia's Asylum **2**
Babe Brandelli's Brig **15**
Bob Burn's Restaurant **3**
Bob Henry's Round Table **8**
The Brewhouse **4**
Circle Bar **11**
Cyber Java **14**
Father's Office **1**

Gotham Hall **6**
Library Ale House **10**
Oar House **9**
O'Brien's Irish Pub & Restaurant **7**
Tavern on Main **12**
World Cafe **13**
Ye Olde King's Head **5**

West Hollywood Area Bars

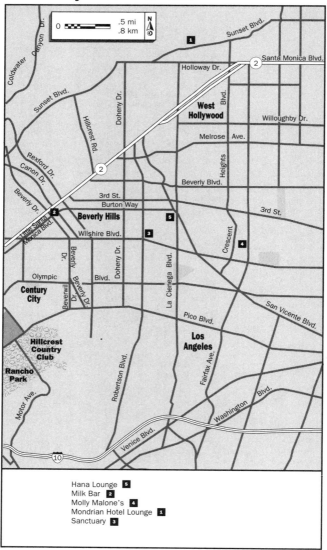

Hana Lounge **5**
Milk Bar **2**
Molly Malone's **4**
Mondrian Hotel Lounge **1**
Sanctuary **3**

Hollywood Area Bars

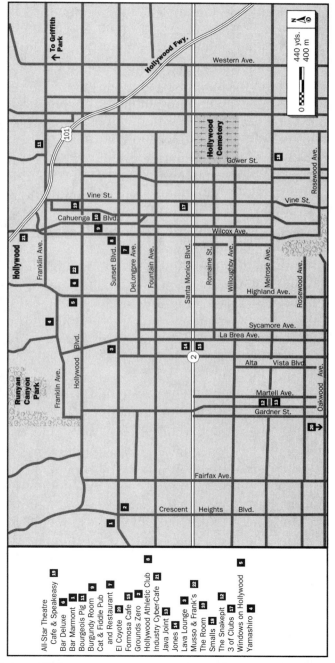

All-Star Theatre **19**
Cafe & Speakeasy **6**
Bar Deluxe **16**
Bar Marmont **11**
Bourgeois Pig **9**
Burgundy Room **7**
Cat & Fiddle Pub and Restaurant **20**
El Coyote **15**
Formosa Cafe **2**
Grounds Zero **8**
Hollywood Athletic Club **21**
Industry Cyber-Cafe **13**
Java Joint **14**
Jones **3**
Lava Lounge **22**
Musso & Frank's **10**
The Room **18**
Smalls **12**
The Snakepit **17**
3 of Clubs **5**
Windows on Hollywood **4**
Yamashiro

the

arts

We don't need no stinkin' culture, *ese*. That's not to say we don't have it here. It's just that with the weather, the beaches, and two-ton sound systems in our cars, we don't need it, and consequently it seems we don't value it, support it, or respect it. Not as entertainment, that is. This doesn't hold true for *Cats*, *Les Miserables*, or other megabudget extravaganzas. Those are Events, like the Rose Parade or the Superbowl, whose opening nights bring out the well-heeled in droves, clogging the streets as they line up for valet parking. And in L.A., anything that stops traffic gets noticed eventually.

With film, TV, and popular-music production dominating so much of the public's awareness, it's no surprise that those *other* performance arts—theater, dance, and opera—get ignored. Sure, the local print media covers them, but about the only time you see a mention of classical music on local TV is for the annual Fourth of July fireworks and *1812 Overture* hoopla at the Hollywood Bowl. You don't see too many paparazzi hanging outside the little experimental theaters on Santa Monica Boulevard. Or, for that matter, outside the Music Center either, unless the Oscars are happening.

But somehow, even as we lose football teams, we manage to slog along culturally, growing up inch by inch, even if we're unwilling to admit it. The pivotal point was probably the 1984 Olympic Arts Festival, when troublemaker extraordinaire Peter Sellers brought artists and provocateurs from all over the world to the Southland for what seemed like an endless multiethnic party. Suddenly it seemed like Los Angeles had arrived. These long pants *do* fit, we thought, and while you can't break-dance in them, they look kinda cool.

The salad days didn't last long, unfortunately, as our baser instincts resurfaced on "America's Most Wanted" home videos starring Rodney King, the L.A.P.D., and a cast of thousands, looting and burning their way to stardom. Who needs fireworks at the Bowl when the whole city's on fire? Ironically, the riots and the uncomfortable self-examination that followed was good for the arts scene, forcing belated acknowledgment that L.A. is a multiethnic city, not just a string of disconnected suburbs linked by freeways. Los Angeles may be dysfunctional, like every good American family, but at least now we don't sit pouting in our rooms when there's an argument. If you don't believe it, check out what's happening at the smaller theaters, at the spoken-word readings, at film revival houses. Angelenos may not agree on just what good culture is, but we're willing to visit new neighborhoods to see what passes for it there.

The relative health and variety of the live theater scene in Los Angeles surprises many people who assume L.A. is all bland, packaged entertainment, with airheads talking on their cell phones during the third act. Well, it *is*, actually, but even so, some drama critics say more small-theater possibilities exist here than in any other city in the country. And that includes the Big Apple. The small houses may not make any money, but who cares? All those actors need a place to work while they wait for that role of a lifetime in some big-budget Demi Moore whore-with-a-heart-of-gold tearjerker or "Friends"-meets-"Frasier" sitcom.

This means a bonanza for culture vultures on a budget. Smaller theater venues are scattered throughout the city but are most visible on the stretch of Santa Monica Boulevard in Hollywood known as Theater Row. Don't expect bright lights or rows of limos here, however. The largely anonymous the-aters are hard to pick out from the surrounding storefronts, auto-body shops, liquor stores, and junk-food joints. You'll have a hard time finding parking spaces, but the neighborhood is totally safe. L.A.'s true cultural life surfaces here; it's street-level, accessible, and it reflects the mélange of cultures in L.A. There is a certain freedom in exploring creativity outside of the pressure cooker of New York, one which has been especially beneficial for artists, directors, actors, curators, dancers, and writers. Don't be surprised to see a cross-pollinating of disci-plines and a tendency to take risks that sometimes work, some-times don't.

Tickets, Seats, Programs

Probably the most essential ticket source for local stage activ-ity is **Theatre L.A.** (tel 213/688–2787), for information about local theater, dance, music, and festival events along with dis-count ticket contacts. **Tickets L.A.** (tel 213/660–8587) also has ticket information for the smaller theatrical stages, as does **Theatix** (tel 213/466–1767). And don't bother asking about an Equity waiver. The new term is "99-seat plan," even though that may not mean there are 99 seats: It refers to the upper limit of seating for nonunion shows; often such venues have two or three stages operating simultaneously.

The Lowdown

Top of the cultural food chain... Where would L.A. be without the **Music Center of Los Angeles County**? Well, besides having an extra 7 acres of prime Bunker Hill real estate, we probably wouldn't have an opera, the ultimate high-water mark for a city's cultural maturity. This enormous three-stage facility is strategically located in the heart of downtown, far enough from skid row to discourage all but the most intrepid panhandlers, but close enough to the freeways for a quick escape back to the west side and the Valley. It's the home of L.A.'s big three: the **Mark Taper Forum**, **Dorothy Chandler Pavilion**, and **Ahmanson Theatre**. It will eventually house the Walt Disney Concert Hall, the future permanent residence of the Los Angeles Philharmonic. (No time soon, unfortunately; the parking garage is done, but the facility itself probably won't open for four or five years.) Now the Philharmonic plays in the Pavilion, as do the Los Angeles Opera and the Master Chorale. Huge and oddly Stalinesque, the Pavilion feels something like the ballroom of the Titanic—just before the iceberg. Seating 3,000, it manages to be comfortable and oppressive at the same time, which I guess was Buffy Chandler's idea of what high culture should be.

Half as big but more enjoyable, the Ahmanson completed a $17 million yearlong face-lift in 1995, gutting the theater and expanding its staging and seating capabilities. Now it seats 1,300 to 2,000, depending on the production. This is where you'll see those ever-popular big-budget musicals like *Miss Saigon* and *Sunset Boulevard*. I'd hardly call it cozy, but it is a far superior viewing experience compared to the Pavilion. On the bottom rung is the Mark Taper Forum, featuring a semicircular stage and great viewing angles. More experimental events crop up here, though you shouldn't expect to see something that would really offend you. This *is* the Music Center, after all.

In Hollywood, the **Pantages Theater** has something that the Music Center lacks—a sense of history. Built in 1930 as classy movie house, it reflects the glory and excess of the era, boasting a lobby that feels like something out of *Gone With the Wind*, a massive stage, and the atmosphere of a real theater experience, even in the balcony. The incredible production values here unfortunately don't offset the neighborhood—but an evening at the theater should include a little personal drama, like wondering if your radio will still be there when you get back to the car. Like the Ahmanson, big-budget musicals are a staple here.

Over in Century City in the shadow of the twin towers, there's the **Shubert Theatre**. Located in a three-deck mall-like entertainment center, it's an L.A. classic that showcases big-budget touring musicals. It seats more than 2,000 and is built on Century City scale—that is, humongous. Some seats are lousy and the general ambience is a little sterile, but the production values are top-notch.

Finally, don't forget about Glendale. The **Alex Theatre** is located on notoriously sleepy Brand Boulevard. It's right down the street from *the* Galleria—the one that spawned valley girls—but don't let that stop you. A wonderful 1920s movie palace that now hosts musicals, opera, and big-budget plays, it has a great feel. The production values are state-of-the-art, but they can't compete with the glorious Greek and Egyptian motifs that define the space. It is one of the last surviving examples of a grand vaudeville venue, a true treasure. Among the groups that work out of the Alex are the Glendale Symphony Orchestra, the Los Angeles Chamber Orchestra, and the Gay Men's Chorus of Los Angeles.

Easy 99-seat pickings... With a built-in connection to working screen actors—Holly Hunter was one of the co-founders—the **Met Theatre** is a nice open space, versatile in its staging possibilities, and has the best viewing choices around. The productions range from old radio dramas to West Coast debuts by established New York writers, often starring familiar famous faces in the leads. In a similar vein, at least in terms of its reputation, is **The Matrix Theatre**, headed by veteran Joseph Stern, probably one of the ten most influential people in local theater. Under his guidance, the Melrose-area venue exudes confidence, winning awards both for its original works as well as for revivals. Living up to its name, the **West Coast Ensemble Theater** features a loose-knit crew of 200. Some major actors have emerged from their midst, most recently Jennifer Jason Leigh. They put on contemporary dramas, late-night weirdness, improv, and classics. There are two stages, one with around 80 seats, the other about 55, and both are raked, putting the audience right into the middle of the action. Major local actors like to come here to see and be seen. They've also won *lots* of awards.

Running second only to the Music Center in numbers of patrons served, the **Odyssey Theater** has been a major force in L.A. 99-seat theater since 1969. And it continues to pack them in to its three stages. They do everything from rediscovered classics to contemporary premiers, and are not afraid to put on something that might attract controversy. Theirs is a rotating group of ensemble actors, but they really draw from the whole city. The spaces are beyond basic black box, with high ceilings, comfortable seats, and excellent sight lines.

Right in the heart of Melrose is the **Zephyr Theater**, one of the oldest Equity theaters in the city. For the last three years they've been renovating, most recently overhauling the entire interior and putting in new seats. There's a very pleasant outdoor courtyard as well. The Zephyr is primarily a rental house that brings in productions from all over the country, but their original productions (Mondays through Wednesdays) are a good nonweekend bet. And since you're smack in the middle of Melrose, the shopping and after-theater dining choices are overwhelming. The **Company of Angels Theater** in Silver Lake is one of the oldest small ensemble theaters in the city. Located on a laid-back stretch of Hyperion Avenue, it has a history of presenting strong one-act plays, late-night sketch comedy, and children's theater. It is a true community theater with reasonable production values, comfortable new seating, and a minimal stage.

Beyond the fringe... As the name suggests, the productions at the **Open Fist Theatre Company** aren't your

LOS ANGELES ◟ THE ARTS

standard fare. It's an alternative underground space that, thankfully, doesn't take itself seriously. Their late-night shows on Saturdays are especially… um… *delightful.* (How else would you describe a play about men's desire to menstruate?) They do things here you couldn't even whisper about at the Mark Taper. Their Sunday show, *The Poe Zone,* is also enjoyable, sort of an open-mike mishmash for anybody with a good story to tell or an embarrassing emotion to discharge. This is what all theater should be like in my opinion.

On Cahuenga, **Theatre/Theater** puts on an always-reliable set of known and unknown pieces—performance art to comedy to improv. Their prices are low (averaging $10–15), and they try to have something going seven nights a week. It's not a blind, scattershot approach though. They know what they're doing. Four of their productions have gone on to become movies, another dozen have been optioned. Since it's a comfortable place to explore actor-driven projects, the facility has a very strong following among industry actors, directors, and casting agents. It's low-budget but high-profile, a great launching pad for talent both on and off the stage. Be sure to check out their late-night shows on Fridays and Saturdays.

Without a net (improv)… Without a doubt, the king of ensemble improvisational comedy in L.A. is the resident Groundlings at **The Groundlings Theatre**. From their Melrose Avenue 99-seater, the troupe has fostered scads of comics who have gone on to high-profile careers. It's our own Second City, and one of the most enjoyable and unpredictable audience-participation outings available. Pee Wee Herman's "Playhouse" started off here as a skit, and featured Phil Hartman. You get the idea. They've dominated the improv scene here for so long it's no doubt good that they have a rival now, the Acme Players at the **Acme Comedy Theatre**. Some call them the "new Groundlings," but that's not fair to either troupe. The Acme skits are more scripted than the chaos you might encounter at the Groundlings; their material leans more heavily towards theater than the hit-or-miss intensity of improv.

Finally, there's **Comedy Sportz**, now in their eighth year. This is a totally different form of improv. There are no sketches, no skits, it's 100 percent improv, with suggestions coming from the audience. The humor is played out just like a game. The thirty comics (or "actelets") wear uniforms, play against the clock on Astroturf, and get points for being funny. And there are fouls: *waffling* (if the improv seems to be going nowhere), *blocking* (if the actor refuses to take an audience suggestion), *brown bag* (if the actor crosses the delicacy line and uses material that is not family friendly, a paper bag is put on his/her head), and *groaner* (in which the audience can force the actor to apologize if it just isn't funny).

Reinventing the classics... In a trend-conscious city like L.A., cutting-edge is what gets the notices, but Glendale's **A Noise Within** company earns its respect the old-fashioned way—by doing the classics, some well known, others rare gems. On the third floor of a landmark Masonic temple, the space has converted pews, making it not as comfy as the **Shubert** but a memorable theater experience nonetheless. They don't reinterpret to the point of absurdity or slavishly follow tradition, but work a broad middle ground that continues to offer surprises, basically letting the work speak for itself. Sets are minimal, costumes lavish, lighting excellent. Every season they decide on a theme which they link to the productions; for example, "Blinding Visions," examinations of heroes in an epiphanic moment, or "Relative Encounters," what makes a family work—or not.

For American plays... The **Hudson Theatre** has made a name for itself (and won a fistful of awards from everyone from the NAACP to L.A. drama critics) for its reliance on homegrown authors. It helps that the place is well designed, giving a great raked view of the stage from every seat, and pays attention to little niceties—like adequate sound. There's also a second space, **Hudson Backstage**, which is less snooty in tone, both in physical setup and choice of plays.

Far out... The first resident professional sign-language theater west of the Mississippi, **Deaf West Theatre** is where writers, actors, directors, and designers come to hone their chops within the medium of the American Sign Language. Both classic and contemporary plays are presented, some created expressly for the D.W.T. And no, you don't have to know A.S.L. to enjoy a play here, since simultaneous voice translation is also offered. And parents take note: They also have a children's theater, featuring child actors.

The only theater company in Los Angeles that is dedicated solely to the production of gay and lesbian plays is the **Celebration Theatre**. Now 15 years old, this 64-seater has won awards from *Drama-Logue* and the *L.A. Weekly*. The focus is on positive images of gay lifestyles. For many the locale should be familiar, behind where the old Gay and Lesbian Community Services Center used to be. What makes a play? Is it the costumes, the sets, the lighting, the stage direction? If you think it all comes down to the basics—the words and acting—the **L.A. Theatre Works** radio theater series is for you. The shows are broadcast by KCRW 89.9FM, but it's even better coming to their readings at the Doubletree Hotel. They feature lots of name stars: John Lithgow, Tyne Daly, Lindsay Crouse, JoBeth Williams. One of the most unusual but involving theater choices you could make.

Damaged by art... Even through these times of mean-spirited funds cutting, **LACE** (Los Angeles Contemporary Exhibitions) still manages to provide shows that threaten the status quo. It might be videos, conceptual art, or performances that tell you much more about the human condition than you bargained for. Here's where you see alternately playful, depressing, and beguiling street art—like an installation of hundreds of teddy bears made out of beer cans—by young artists who will be working for the studios in ten years. Appropriately enough, it's smack in the middle of Hollywood, pedestrian friendly for tourists and Scientologists.

Highways Performance Space, in Santa Monica, is only a few years old but has carved out a niche for itself by putting on the most adventuresome and challenging shows around, transcending theater, dance, performance art, and literature to produce something quite unique—an ongoing site for pushing the envelope. There's no predicting what you'll see here—maybe a cervical self-examination display by porn star/performance maven Annie Sprinkle, or self-mutilation rituals from HIV-positive tribal shaman Ron Athey. The focus is intercultural and L.A.-based, working especially strongly with the gay and lesbian community, Latinos, and Asian Americans. The facility is a 110-seat black box. Trivia tidbit: Judy Chicago created her *Dinner Party* piece in this space.

Smells like New York... There are two theater spaces at the **Actor's Gang**, a 99-seater and a second 30-seater that's been around since 1981. But no matter which one you're in, the action will be in your face. This well-known, respected venue is home to working TV and film actors, directors, and designers who feel the need to do something *real*, something that's not on tape. The influences include expressionism and commedia dell'arte, and even though the classics are exposed, they're not dealt with reverentially. Scripts alternate between original and previously produced works. Dress up. You're in for a very *theatrical* experience. Most of the shows are developed inhouse for the 45-person ensemble; these productions have legs and travel well.

On Theater Row, you'll find **The Complex**. It's aptly named, boasting five stages, all with heat, air-conditioning, raked seating, proscenium stages, and weathered but not wrecked facilities. Although all the theaters are on the small side (between 42 and 55 seats), only Theatre 6470 has the black-walled claustrophobic feel. Eclectic, democratic, informal, multiethnic in feel, they've won numerous awards for their productions. It is truly a complex, with rehearsal studios, offices, audition spaces, a real bustle and buzz. It feels like New York, say many.

Another 99-seater with a big New York vibe is the **Coast Playhouse**, a 30-year-old theater that has recently gotten a big shot in the arm with the arrival of new producer/owner D.W. Fairbanks. With a background in and ongoing connection to theater in Manhattan, he knows what he's looking for: drama, musicals, or performance art that either comes from New York or is on its way there. If he doesn't find something that holds up, then he just leaves the theater dark. This is not a vanity showcase. Basically, you'll find an eclectic mix of new material. If it's a traveling show, there's an effort to have the original cast and/or writers directly involved—not always the case in other L.A. venues.

The **Attic Theatre** is a space that actors like, even though it's small (53 seats in the main stage, 44 in the **Attic Too**, upstairs). They do everything from original one acts to classics, spicing things up with color- and gender-blind casting.

Pacific rim shots... The oldest Asian theater troupe in the country, the **East West Players** has spent thirty years turning immigrant experiences into top-notch theater. This 99-seater is not just a one-trick pony, however, as evidenced by its recent entire season devoted to female writers or actors in lead roles.

On a far grander scale, seemingly from another economy altogether, is the **Japan America Theatre** in Little Tokyo. The room is architecturally stunning, large (841 seats), sports a sound system of deadly strength, and has supercomfortable seats (and be warned—Kabuki is one of the strongest soporifics known to man). The clientele is older, sophisticated, and well-heeled. This is the best (and only) outlet for genuine Japanese theater, ranging from No to Butoh.

Recent arrivals... Like green shoots after a brushfire, new theater seems to crop up in Los Angeles with self-denying regularity. Haven't they heard? L.A. isn't a theater town. *Everyone* says so. Well, don't tell the people at the **Wolfskill Theater**, a community theater in the downtown artists' ghetto. It's located in a former transient hotel, appropriately enough, and named after an Angeleno immigrant who planted the first orange orchards here. Whether or not it takes root seems to be up to the community. There's a wealth of talent in the lofts nearby, mainly industry professionals who are willing to donate time and effort to make this black box work as a community resource, not as a showcase runway. It's a little early to say what the dominant theme of the facility will be, but one thing's for certain—the sets will look great.

Then over in Culver City, there's **ESPACE DbD**, dancer/performance artist Rachel Rosenthal's private laboratory. Rosenthal has been a thorn in the side of the established fine-arts scene in L.A. for years, an animal-rights activist long before it was a trendy movement. And like her politics, her work can be difficult but is never compromised. In the fifties she started a company called Instant Theatre which labored on through the seventies but was gradually overshadowed by her solo prominence. She's continued teaching workshops and classes from this facility on South Robertson Boulevard, and now the ensemble has started public shows. Nonverbal, focusing on movement and emotional improvisation, her most recent production, *Toho Bohu!*, was nonlinear, non-narrative, and surreal in style. A balcony hangs over the performance space, so watch your head.

Both geographically and aesthetically, Silver Lake's **Glaxa Studios** is halfway between the small "real" theater houses on Santa Monica Boulevard in Hollywood and the art-damaged lofts of downtown. Termed "The Best Community Performance Space" by the *L.A. Weekly*, this high-ceilinged box on Sunset is perfectly suited to the neighborhood, putting on shows that are kinda twisted, kinda kinky, but always interesting.

For cineastes... Here in Los Angeles we take film seriously. So seriously that yes, just about everyone is working on a screenplay and no, nobody really believes that star-making-machinery, magic-of-the-silver-screen nonsense. The cement imprints at Mann's Chinese Theater are for *tourists*. Once you've had a production crew take all the parking on your block or make you late for an appointment while the PAs drink Perrier and wait for the star to get in the mood, you begin to wonder how you too could climb onto the back of this bloated, overfed beast. Call it *the business* or *the industry*. It doesn't matter as long as you're part of it. I mean Quentin Tarantino was working in a video store not too long ago, and now he's got a whole clone section in the budget rentals.

The most consistently interesting film series in the city takes place at the **Bing Theater** at the Los Angeles County Museum of Art. It's not your typical movie experience, but you can bet nobody will be crackling candy wrappers during the film. The audience here is more interested in what's happening on screen than what they're putting in their mouths. The facilities are state-of-the-art, and the retrospectives regularly sell out to enthusiastic crowds. They will cover the work of a director like Sam Pekinpah, of an actor, or of a studio genre.

LOS ANGELES ⟅ THE ARTS

Once or twice a month, if that, the Academy of Motion Picture Arts and Sciences hosts public screenings of Oscar-winning classics at their cushy 1,000-seat **Samuel Goldwyn Theater**. The price is right—either free or just a few dollars—and no, you don't have to be a member of the Academy. Again, no popcorn.

And you don't have to be a student to delve into the extensive collection of rare and classic films, art and documentary shorts at the UCLA Film and Television Archive. Screenings take place on the campus in the **Melnitz Theatre**, a pleasant Dolby sound–equipped venue. Besides films in their collection, they also present independent productions. For historians, their summer Festival of Preservation is a must, featuring films whose prints have been rescued from degradation.

For true lovers of cinema, the **American Cinematheque** organization is one-stop shopping. They feature tributes, revivals, independent debuts, and art projects, and often follow up the screenings with discussions with producers or directors. All their screenings are open to the public—you don't have to be a member—and the board of directors includes a bunch of industry heavy hitters like Sidney Pollack. Think of the Film Forum in New York and you get the idea. Right now their screenings are being held at the Raleigh Studios on Melrose. They try to be "an alternative to your local cineplex," but they're way more significant than that. You'll see films and projects here you've never heard of but should have.

The IMAX experience... The most impressive screen experience in L.A. has nothing to do with Hollywood, ironically. It's the **IMAX Theater**, down in Exposition Park, near USC. It's part of the Museum of Science and Technology, and while the films don't have much character development, the technology used packs enough of a punch that you won't worry about plotlines. Think *National Geographic*, but on a screen that's five stories high and 70 feet wide, with film frames that are ten times normal size. This is the most intense film experience you'll ever have.

Midnight cult-movie madness... Don't ask me to explain the fascination with *The Rocky Horror Picture Show*. Like polyester, Rush Limbaugh, or disco, it's a force of nature. A phenomenon that defies evolution. It will not die. And for the faithful—your numbers are legion—the mecca of screen mockery has to be the **Nuart Theatre**, easily the most interesting revival screen in Los Angeles. Of course their *Rocky Horror* events (Saturdays at midnight) are not exactly revivals, since the film never left. For those who can't handle the drive across town, there's a similar *Rocky Horror* talk-back-fest happening in Pasadena at the historic (and classy, if a bit run-down) **Rialto Theatre**, also at midnight on Saturdays. The **New Beverly Cinema** is also working the cult circuit, although in a slightly more modern vein. This was L.A.'s first art house back in the 1970s, and it hasn't seen much improvement over the years. Their current Saturday night regular is *Reservoir Dogs*, the choice of a new generation.

Lovers of Japanese *manga* videos have the perfect venue in which to enjoy these bizarre futuristic animated films—**Fatburger**, the home of the greasiest, sloppiest burger in the city. The West Hollywood Fatburger plays the videos on three large-screen TVs scattered around the room. The marriage of meat and *manga* is so brilliant I expect to see it copied elsewhere. (See Late Night Dining.)

Silents... Built in 1942, the 250-seat **Silent Movie** theater in the Fairfax District is the world's only venue built expressly for the screening of nontalkies (although you wouldn't know it from the lobby, where you'll find the typical movie munchies—popcorn, candy, and sodas). The films come from a variety of sources like UCLA, the Eastman archives, and Ted Turner's library, and are accompanied by live organ music. At the end of August they hold a festival of rare and forgotten gems. Charlie Chaplin used to come here. **The Silent Society** at the Hollywood Studio Museum, across from the Hollywood Bowl, is another good spot for silents, although with a much less frequent schedule.

Concerts al fresco... L.A. may have the liveliest club scene on the West Coast, but let's face it, being crowded into the corner of a smoke-filled bar by boorish drunks isn't always conducive to appreciating music. Maybe that's why you never see opera or chamber music on the

Strip. That's not to say that classical music is anathema to Hollywood. After all, the most famous classical pops venue in California is just up the Cahuenga Pass from Hollywood Boulevard: **The Hollywood Bowl**.

Summertime is the time for Bowl-ing, either packing your own picnic or buying one from the vendors lined up outside. Built in the 1920s and with seating for 18,000 plus, the Bowl is one of the city's major icons (right up there with Mickey Mouse, the freeways, and City Hall). The choice seats are in the boxes in front of the amphitheater's band shell. The back benches and grassy area are cheaper and more for the ambience than the sound. And even though the acoustics here can be erratic (due to the dimensions, the sometimes misty conditions in the Cahuenga Pass, and the annoying, ever-present police helicopters), it's an evening unlike any other, even if you don't know Bartok from Bach. Subscribers here greedily hold on to their private boxes, passing them from one generation to the next as cherished legacies. The card here runs the gamut, from jazz to classical to Broadway musicals. It's middlebrow mayhem, especially when the parking situation gets out of control (as it almost always does) and that picnic box is starting to feel extraordinarily heavy. Did you really *need* the silver candelabra?

Far cozier in size, but without the tony vibe, is **The Greek Theatre**, right at the entrance to Griffith Park. It seats just over 6,000 and is not a picnic-to-the-pops kind of place. Touring rock, jazz, and pop stars play here, May through October. From the outside, the faux-Greek facade is kind of cheesy but the sound inside is good, the seats more or less comfortable, and the sight lines great from just about everywhere. Even if you're sitting in the back, the sound system is powerful enough to lift you off your seat. This is hot-date heaven. Be warned, though: The parking situation here is a killer. Give yourself plenty of time to walk down the hill.

Right across the Cahuenga Pass from the Hollywood Bowl you'll find the **John Anson Ford Amphitheater**, funky, small and completely endearing. It also dates from the 1920s and is the total opposite of its neighbor across the way. Rustic and seating about 1,200, this is the closest thing to a community-based amphitheater that exists around here. Everything from classical music to opera to neopunk and experimental theater can be found here. It's operated by the County Parks and Recreation Department, and rented out to whomever, so the sound and general production values can vary wildly. It's a great space, regardless of the quality of the production, with a genuine old-California feel.

The most underappreciated amphitheater in the city has to be the **Remsen Bird Hillside Theater**, on the campus of Occidental College in Eagle Rock. It seats 3,500—uncomfortably, unfortunately, due to the hard, cold concrete construction—and offers an interesting if predictable mix of classic drama and musicals.

Arena agony... Although basketball fans know the **Great Western Forum** in Inglewood as the home of the Lakers, for too many hapless fans this is the epitome of arena rock. When they cover the floor and bring in seats it can hold 18,000. And too often it does. The huge circular building rises like a toadstool after a rain in the middle of a giant parking lot. The sound is wretched unless you're right down in front on the floor.

Readings, writings, ravings... The spoken-word mania that so dominates coffeehouse spaces should not discourage you from going back to the source. There's an authenticity in bookstore readings and lectures that just isn't present when you're slouching comfortably on a beaten-up sofa, sipping a double latte. And if the words being spoken leave you cold, you can browse the stacks and find something on a page that's more to your liking.

It's hard to imagine a more stereotypical L.A. bookstore than the **Bodhi Tree** in West Hollywood. On their monthly flyers to customers, detailing upcoming events, fully one quarter is given over to parking instructions ("where you can always park, park most of the time, never park"). This store is New Age Central, packed floor to ceiling with books dealing with everything from auras to Zen, plus CDs, incense, and self-betterment accessories. There are readings and workshops throughout the week, ranging from "Introduction to Feng Shui" to "The Feldenkrais Method." (If you don't know, don't ask.) Some are free, while others, like the 12-part "Artist's Way" workshop, can cost. And west-siders won't have to cross Robertson to get their chakras realigned. Santa Monica's contribution to the harmonic convergence is the **Phoenix Bookstore**. It offers much of the same, but without quite the same preciousness.

Also out in Santa Monica you'll find **L.A. (The Bookstore)**, which is dedicated to all things in print relating to L.A. It's a peculiar idea but one that works. They sponsor poetry and spoken-word readings, and will overwhelm you with the quantity of material here, both fiction and non-fiction. Hard to imagine that so much has been written about and in a city that supposedly doesn't read. Further north, on the Promenade, the **Midnight Special Bookstore** offers a wonderful escape from the frenzy outside, complete with wooden floors and an overall bibliophile ambience that would do New York proud. Again, it has poetry and spoken-word readings. The floor-to-ceiling collection has everything from classics to the latest bestsellers and the cream of undiscovered new voices. Down in Venice, in the old Venice City Hall, is the most important multi-purpose facility for creative writers in L.A., **Beyond Baroque**. It hosts regular readings and workshops by poets and writers of every genre. The reading space is minimalist at best—black walls and folding seats from hell—but you're feeding your mind, not your butt. The bookstore across the hall contains one of the largest small-press (fiction and non-fiction) and poetry selections found anywhere in L.A. They have a full range of the tiny Hanuman books on sale, but unfortunately the great collection of pulp paperbacks behind the front desk is not for sale. There are readings every Friday night, most Saturdays, and free writing workshops Mondays, Wednesdays, and Thursdays. The bookstore is generally open until 10:30pm when there are performances. For writings about gay and lesbian topics, the G-spot is **A Different Light** in West Hollywood. It's about the only place to browse and cruise at the same time, although the latter is not required. Poetry readings, writing workshops, and readings of new work are held regularly. **Sisterhood Bookstore** in Westwood is another specialty outlet, concentrating on books by, for, and about women. They also host readings and group discussions (third Thursday of the month).

Finally, over on the Sunset Strip, across from Tower Records, is **Book Soup**, about the only reason I'd ever consider moving to West Hollywood. This is the bookstore of my dreams: a mammoth magazine selection, loads of hardbacks, hard-to-find weirdos and malcontents, and a selection that usually covers an author's entire career, not just the latest best-seller. Plus readings, book signings, and fairly frequent celebrity spottings. If you can't find something to read here, you're not really looking.

Family fun... Is making beer an art? Don't answer that until you've swung by the do-it-yourself brewery **Brew 'n' Case**. As the owner says, "If you can boil water, you can make beer." The sterile setting—dominated by a large worktable (flash back to high school chemistry) and a row of stainless-steel kettles—is not exactly ideal for a first date, but it's better than watching TV. And when it's time for bottling, *then* you can invite your friends to help out and make a party of it. They have more than 100 recipes to choose from and you'll get all the help you need in measuring extracts and flavorings to be added to your brew. After the two-week fermentation, you'll wind up with six cases of 24-ounce bottles (13.5 gallons). Average cost is $110, about $4.75 a six-pack. And you know what you're drinking. The last brew starts at 8pm and the doors close between 10 and 11, depending on activity.

Also in Pasadena but less spirited is **Mudd Beach**, a combination art gallery and ceramics studio where you pick out the shape you like (already made) and then apply the glazes, designs, and paints of your choice. Open until 11pm Friday and Saturday.

And who said *you* aren't an artiste, another Pavarotti, maybe? To find out, there's **Karaoke Fantasy** in Little Tokyo, where you can indulge your hard-beltin' vocalizations to the absolute limit of physical endurance. This is where you hone your song stylings in a private room before you hit the big time—that karaoke bar down the street where some of the singers don't even have to look at the lyric sheet. The facilities here are CD-driven, and there's a range of special effects to choose from to achieve that *perfect* Meatloaf-like quality: reverb, echo, pitch control, and the like. There are nearly 8,000 song titles to choose from, although more than half are in Asian languages (Japanese, Korean, Thai, Indonesian, and Filipino). What's more, you can take home a video of your stunning performance for the folks back home.

Probably the best thing about the **Laserium** show is its location, in the wonderful **Griffith Observatory**. The light and sound shows take place in the Planetarium, the huge domed theater in the Observatory, for my money the natural home for a Pink Floyd soundtrack. More interesting, but less dramatic, are the Planetarium's star map displays put on prior to Laserium for a separate charge. They last about an hour and offer an astronomical education that won't put you to sleep. For those on a budget, the Hall of Science and the Observatory's 12-inch telescope are both free to the public. There's always a line for the latter so wander around the hall and inspect their meteorites, the Cosmic Ray Cloud Chamber, or see what you'd weigh on Jupiter. Lots of parking and a wonderful view of the city from the walkways outside.

The Index

Acme Comedy Theater. Are they Groundlings Too? Not really. The structure is slightly different and the profile not nearly as high—but it is improv.... *Tel 213/525–0202. 135 N. La Brea Ave., Hollywood.*

Actor's Gang. The space here is relatively new, two stages and a concentrated effort to walk the fine line between cutting edge and classical. Usually they succeed, reworking older pieces to fit the ensemble or creating totally original scripts that will probably wind up in New York. Check out their late-night shows on the weekends.... *Tel 213/465–0566. 6209 Santa Monica Blvd., Hollywood.*

Ahmanson Theatre. Recently refurbished to the tune of $17 million, this home away from home for touring big-budget musicals and important stage productions is the top of the heap.... *Tel 213/972–7401. At the Music Center, 135 N. Grand Ave., Downtown.*

Alex Theatre. This Glendale landmark is a beautiful space, seating 1,450 and with production values that are state-of-the-art. Recently renovated, it plays host to musicals, big-budget dramas, opera, chorales, chamber music, and symphonies. This is the brightest spot on Glendale's cultural map.... *Tel 818/243–7700. 216 N. Brand Blvd., Glendale.*

American Cinematheque. This is a member-supported film appreciation society that screens some of the best and rarest films you've never heard of. They have foreign festivals, local independent projects, art-house flicks, classics. If it's on celluloid, it'll eventually wind up here. Plus you get to go onto a studio lot to see the films so you know the seats are comfy.... *Tel 213/466–3456. Screenings now* *being held at the Charlie Chaplin Theater, Raleigh Studios, 5300 Melrose Ave., Hollywood.*

Attic Theatre/Attic Too. Two spaces: one proscenium, the other thrust. There are good sight lines in both, but not the most comfortable of seats. Lots of name actors have studied here— Patrick Swayze and Michelle Pfeiffer to name two. Contemporary works to classics and right in the heart of Theater Row.... *Tel 213/469–3786. 6562½ Santa Monica Blvd., Hollywood.*

Beyond Baroque. Not quite as literary an establishment as San Francisco's City Lights, this very-Venice bookstore/performance space does its best to support local writers, readers, and weirdos. An essential resource. Open until 10:30 on event nights.... *Tel 310/822–3006. 681 Venice Blvd., Venice.*

Bing Theater. Easily the most comfortable and serious place to see films that make a difference. Be warned: no *Terminator* or *Rocky* series. Also no popcorn.... *Tel 213/857–6010. 5905 Wilshire Blvd. (at the Los Angeles County Museum of Art), Mid-Wilshire.*

Bodhi Tree. More than a bookstore, less than a Learning Annex, it's the New Age incarnate. Incense, self-help, soul rebirthing.... *Tel 310/659–1733. 8585 Melrose Ave., West Hollywood.*

Book Soup. This is the best bookstore, hands down, in the entire city. The evening readings and book signings are just icing on the cake. Hollywood doesn't deserve a bookstore this good. Open until midnight.... *Tel 310/659–3110. 8818 Sunset Blvd., West Hollywood.*

Brew 'n' Case. This state-of-the-art brew-your-own-beer facility comes from a trend that is superpopular in Canada and is just now coming to the U.S. This is only the second such outlet in Southern California. Plan on 90 minutes to make your batch and then returning a few weeks later for bottling. That's when the fun begins.... *Tel 818/583–9087. 79 N. Raymond Ave., Pasadena.*

Celebration Theatre. This is the only theater in Los Angeles that solely produces plays with gay or lesbian themes.

Winner of awards for best actor, ensemble, writer, director.... *Tel 213/957–1884. 7051B Santa Monica Blvd., West Hollywood.*

Coast Playhouse. Large, comfortable, and air conditioned with a broad palette to chose from, this is the closest you'll get to a hard-core New York vibe. Performance art to musicals, original casts of touring productions. Quality work.... *Tel 213/650–8509. 8325 Santa Monica Blvd., West Hollywood.*

Comedy Sportz. Interactive improv that brings the audience in as referee. An interesting idea, if a little bloodlessly executed.... *Tel 213/871–1193. At Tamarind Theatre, 5919 Franklin Ave., Hollywood.*

Company of Angels Theatre. This is one of the most venerable theater companies in the city. The sight lines are good, the seats suck, the productions are interesting and socially aware, ranging from classics to originals.... *Tel 213/666–6789. 2106 Hyperion Ave., Silver Lake.*

The Complex. There are five stages here, rehearsal spaces, classes and workshops, and a general frenzy of activity that should make New Yorkers homesick. One of the central anchors of Santa Monica Boulevard's Theatre Row section.... *Tel 213/466–1767. 6476 Santa Monica Blvd., Hollywood.*

Deaf West Theatre. Performances here are signed in American Sign Language and performed by the only resident troupe of deaf actors in the western U.S. Simultaneous voice translation is also offered. A totally unique theater experience.... *Tel 213/660–0877. 660 N. Heliotrope Dr., Los Angeles.*

A Different Light. Basically a gay alternative bookstore, this is also a prime site for readings and contacts that go beyond the cruising scene. Open until midnight.... *Tel 310/854–6601. 8853 Santa Monica Blvd., West Hollywood.*

Dorothy Chandler Pavilion. This is belly of the beast, culturewise, in L.A. Named after *L.A. Times* philanthropist Buffy Chandler, this is the anchor venue for the Music Center. Huge, cavernous, oddly impersonal and remarkably ugly in decor, it does boast great acoustics. Home to the L.A. Phil-harmonic, the Master Chorale, and the Opera.... *Tel 213/850–2000, Philharmonic; 213/972–7282, Master Chorale; 213/972–7219, Music Center Opera. At the Music Center, 135 N. Grand Ave., Downtown.*

East West Players. The most respected and successful Asian/Pacific small theater in L.A., maybe even the country. Strong direction, interesting topics, a so-so space.... *Tel 213/660–0366. 4424 Santa Monica Blvd., Silver Lake.*

ESPACE DbD. This odd little space is performance artist/dancer/animal rights activist Rachel Rosenthal's private workshop. They've just started putting on shows, so the schedule may be spotty. There's a heavy emphasis on improv, dance, emotional expressionism, and chaos.... *Tel 310/839–0661. 2847 S. Robertson Blvd., Los Angeles.*

Glaxa Studios. This is the east side's version of what a performance space should offer to its audience—opinionated and in your face. Don't be put off by the relatively meager production values.... *Tel 213/663–5295. 3707 Sunset Blvd., Silver Lake.*

Great Western Forum. Home of the Lakers, rock bands, big events. Its arena acoustics are about what you'd expect for a place that seats nearly 20,000. Sight lines are generally good. Remember where you parked your car.... *Tel 310/419–3100. 3900 W. Manchester Blvd., Inglewood.*

The Greek Theater. This is one of the joys of living on the east side—you're close to the Greek. Seating around 6,000, this outdoor amphitheater in Griffith Park is a local classic, with good sight, good sound, an aroma of wild sage, and an intimate feel.... *Tel 213/665–1927. 2700 N. Vermont Ave., Los Angeles.*

Griffith Observatory. One of the best (and cheapest) things to do on a warm evening in L.A. is to drive up into the hills and wander through the observatory's Hall of Science and Planetarium. Very child friendly. The planetarium shows last about an hour and cost $4 for adults, $3 for seniors, and $2 for children.... *Tel 213/664–1191 or 213/664–1181. 2800 E. Observatory Rd., Griffith Park.*

LOS ANGELES (THE ARTS

The Groundlings Theatre. Easily the best and most consistent improvisational comedy troupe in the city. Expect lots of audience participation.... *Tel 213/934–4747. 7307 Melrose Ave., Los Angeles.*

Highways Performance Space. The kind of place Pat Buchanan loves to hate. The most consistent performance-art space in the city, this converted warehouse in the industrial section has a more than adequate performance hall but a cramped gallery. It's kind of the unofficial cultural center for the gay and lesbian community but also serves the rest of L.A.... *Tel 310/453–1755. 1651 18th St., Santa Monica.*

Hollywood Bowl. The Amphitheater of the Stars. If Hollywood ever gets a flag, the Bowl should be on it. Jazz, classical, dance, mariachi—the whole L.A. thing.... *Tel 213/972–7300. 2301 N. Highland Ave., Hollywood.*

Hudson Theatre/Hudson Backstage. A very successful and popular pair of stages on Theater Row, it's notable for productions with socially conscious themes. The space is good and production values better than average.... *Tel 213/856–4249. 6539 Santa Monica Blvd., Hollywood.*

IMAX Theater. A *really* big screen that puts sharks, volcanoes, wild animals, and outer space in your face in a way that manages to be educational, nonmanipulative, and terrifying all at the same time. Disneyland should be this good.... *Tel 213/744–2014. Museum of Science and Industry, 700 State Dr. (in Exposition Park, near USC), Los Angeles.*

Japan America Theatre. An absolutely stunning space, this is just about the only place to see new and traditional Japanese performance arts. Prices are high, the audience older and stodgy, but when you've just got to hear those Kodo drummers, this is the place they'll be playing. Great acoustics.... *Tel 213/680–3700. 244 S. San Pedro St., Little Tokyo.*

John Anson Ford Amphitheater. Across the street from the Hollywood Bowl, this is a mini-Bowl for the rest of us. It is small (only 1,200 seats) but it has some of the more interesting events of the summer. Dress warmly.... *Tel 213/974–1343. 2850 Cahuenga Blvd., Hollywood.*

Karaoke Fantasy. Only a handful of rooms available but like any good studio, there's a waiting list. You can even bring your backup group, as long as you've got the cash. It's $25 for one to five people, $40 for six to 13 people. Hey, the more the better! Open until 4am on the weekends, until 2 the rest of the week.... *Tel 213/620–1030. 333 S. Alameda St., #216 (in the Yaohan Plaza facility, second floor), Little Tokyo.*

LACE (Los Angeles Contemporary Exhibitions). A veteran of the downtown art/punk/performance scene, this is a major outlet for mixed-media shows that touch on every discipline but cater to none. An essential space for experimental artists.... *Tel 213/624–5650. 6522 Hollywood Blvd., Hollywood.*

L.A. (The Bookstore). Everything ever written by, for, and about L.A., plus spoken word, comics. An essential resource. Open until 10pm.... *Tel 310/452–2665. 2433 Main St., Santa Monica.*

Laserium. It's where the Beastie Boys, the Beatles, and Beethoven all meet, united in a blaze of lasers. The shows vary every night so call in advance.... *Tel 818/901–9405. Griffith Observatory, 2800 E. Observatory Rd., Griffith Park.*

L.A. Theatre Works. This is theater without the costumes, sets, stage direction, and lights. It's radio drama, acted out by some of the best working actors of the day. An incredibly hypnotic experience.... *Tel 310/827–0889. Held at the Doubletree Guest Suites, 1707 4th St., Santa Monica.*

Mark Taper Forum. One of the most comfortable and well designed theaters in the city, the Taper neatly walks the line between predictable and experimental. This is about as wild as it gets at the Music Center.... *Tel 213/972–7353. At the Music Center, 135 N. Grand Ave., Downtown.*

The Matrix Theatre. A major award-winner in recent years, this 99-seater on Melrose draws name actors.... *Tel 213/653–3279. 7657 Melrose Ave., Los Angeles.*

Melnitz Theatre. Located on the UCLA campus, this is where you can enjoy the university's extensive Film and Television Archives without having to pass a test later. The theater is comfortable and has better sound than my local miniplex.... *Tel 310/206–8013. 1438 Melnitz Hall, 405 Hilgard Ave., Westwood.*

Met Theatre. A 99-seater but with a major connection to the industry, you'll see lots of West Coast premiers here and some famous faces (Dustin Hoffman, Raquel Welch, Holly Hunter) doing their Great Writers series.... *Tel 213/957–1831. 1089 N. Oxford St., Los Angeles.*

Midnight Special Bookstore. It's the best general-interest bookstore on the Promenade, with creaky wooden floors, books floor to ceiling, and poetry and literary events. Despite the name, they close around 11:30 on weekends.... *Tel 310/393–2923. 1318 Third St. Promenade, Santa Monica.*

Mudd Beach. A do-it-yourself ceramics workshop/gallery. Open until 11 Friday and Saturday.... *Tel 818/449–4050. 148 W. Colorado Blvd., Old Town, Pasadena.*

Music Center of Los Angeles County. This huge three-stage complex on Bunker Hill is the original 800-pound gorilla who sets the tone of the cultural party in L.A. Expensive, glitzy, and home to the Ahmanson Theatre, Mark Taper Forum, Dorothy Chandler Pavilion, L.A. Opera, L.A. Master Chorale, and L.A. Philharmonic.... *Tel 213/972–7211. 135 N. Grand Ave., Downtown.*

New Beverly Cinema. This is an oddity, one of the few newer theaters to host midnight shows. And to their credit, their Saturday-night midnight staple is not *Rocky Horror*, but instead, *Reservoir Dogs*.... *Tel 213/938–4038. 7165 Beverly Blvd., Fairfax.*

A Noise Within. This highly respected theater company concentrates on serious classics, from Shakespeare to O'Neill, expertly reinventing and re-creating with a style that is engaging and usually compelling. Seating is on old restored pews. There's a three-quarter thrust and the sets are minimal at best. Costumes and lighting are elaborate. Basically they let the words and the actors do the work—

which is as it should be.... *Tel 818/546–1924. Glendale Masonic Temple, 234 S. Brand Blvd., Glendale.*

Nuart Theatre. Midnight shows on Fridays and Saturdays (*The Rocky Horror Picture Show* on Saturdays). The theater is nothing to rave about, but this is the best revival house in the city. The perfect place to throw candy at the screen and talk back.... *Tel 310/478–6379. 11272 Santa Monica Blvd., West Los Angeles.*

Odyssey Theater. This three-stage facility is one of the top five small theaters in the city, presenting new plays, classics, the occasional late-night event. They're well respected and have won countless drama awards. Seats are comfy, production values way above average. This is not a black-box experience.... *Tel 310/477–2055. 2055 S. Sepulveda Blvd., West Los Angeles.*

Open Fist Theatre Company. Experimental theater, readings, oddities, and weirdness. Never a dull moment, guaranteed.... *Tel 213/882–6912. 1625–27 N. La Brea Ave., Hollywood.*

Pantages Theater. Hardly a relic from the past, this former movie palace is a theater in the old tradition, with a lobby that will knock you out, a wonderfully expansive stage, and great production values. A far more romantic venue for touring musicals than the Ahmanson.... *Tel 213/466–1700. 6233 Hollywood Blvd., Hollywood.*

Phoenix Bookstore. This is Santa Monica's brightest bead on the New Age Rosary. From acupuncture to Zoroaster, lots of spiritual tidbits.... *Tel 310/395–9516. 1514 5th Ave., Santa Monica.*

Remsen Bird Hillside Theater. Eagle Rock has an amphitheater? Located on the Occidental College campus, this small (3,200 seats) concrete facility is cozy and family friendly, perfect for a warm summer night of culture with the kids.... *Tel 213/259–2737. 1600 Campus Road, Echo Park.*

Rialto Theatre. *The Rocky Horror Picture Show* happens Saturdays at midnight. This is an older theater, not a classic, but with a real full-sized screen.... *Tel 8181/799–9567. 1023 Fair Oaks Ave., Pasadena.*

Samuel Goldwyn Theater. Super plush, no treats, open to the public regularly (but not nightly) for screenings of rare and Oscar-winning films, lectures, and talks…. *Tel 310/247–3000. At the Academy of Motion Picture Arts and Sciences, 8949 Wilshire Blvd., Beverly Hills.*

Shubert Theatre. A mammoth yet futile attempt to bring culture to Century City's skyscraper wasteland, this is an okay place for over-the-top musicals but is totally frustrating when it comes to anything that doesn't involve a cast of hundreds…. *Tel 310/201–1500. At the ABC Entertainment Center, 2020 Avenue of the Stars, Century City.*

Silent Movie. This is reportedly the only movie house in the world still in operation that was built expressly for silents. Screenings are accompanied by live organ music. A full snack stand…. *Tel 213/653–2389. 611 N. Fairfax Ave., Fairfax.*

The Silent Society. This is the only other place for regular screenings of silents, although on an infrequent basis…. *Tel 213/874–2276. At the Hollywood Studio Museum, 2100 N. Highland Ave., Hollywood.*

Sisterhood Bookstore. This bookstore dedicated to words about women from Sappho to Andrea Dworkin also hosts evening book-discussion groups and readings. They close at 8pm…. *Tel 310/477–7300. 1351 Westwood Blvd., Westwood.*

Theatre/Theater. A high-profile small theater in Hollywood, the kind of place that puts on well-written plays featuring actors who don't need the work. The play *Creeps* went to New York from here…. *Tel 213/850–6941. 1713 Cahuenga Blvd., Hollywood.*

West Coast Ensemble Theater. Two theaters working the entire range of theatrical choices—classics to comedy, improv to premiers. It's a working actors' hangout and boasts an enormous pool of talent upon which to draw…. *Tel 213/871–8673. 6240 Hollywood Blvd., Hollywood.*

Wolfskill Theater. So new it doesn't really have a reputation yet, this is an effort to create a community-based theater among industry professionals living in the art scene downtown. It's a medium-size black box that's flexible; the idea is to make it a quality space, not a vanity showcase.... *Tel 213/620–9229. 806 E. 3rd. St., Downtown.*

Zephyr Theater. It's the last on the list alphabetically but in no other way. Recently renovated inside, it plays host to traveling productions from everywhere. Recently they've also started producing their own originals Monday through Wednesday.... *Tel 213/653–4667. 7456 Melrose Ave., Hollywood.*

spo

rts

4

For a city where the cult of
the body beautiful was
born and where such an
emphasis is placed on
looking and acting
youthful that even Lolita
might feel like a has-been,

you may wonder why the sporting scene is so fragmented. Sure, the Dodgers play for a profit every season, but the fans are legendary for leaving early, even during a tight game. And in the last year, L.A. has lost not one but two professional football teams. Instead, it has one great basketball team, its terrible counterpart, and a shoulda-been-a-contender hockey team.

Many sports fans in L.A. just don't display the rabid intensity about their teams that you find in other major cities. Maybe it's because people here are more concerned with their own personal stats than with some overpriced twentysomething star athlete with a substance-abuse problem. The weather here encourages people to do it themselves, to be their own champions in their own fantasies—maybe at the urging of their own professional trainer. Even at night. Not everybody sees twilight as a time to get dressed and wonder about where to have that first martini. For some it's the right time to hit the courts, the trails, the lanes, the fields, or—if they want to kick back—the bleachers.

The Lowdown

Where to watch

Pigskin... Go **Raiders**! What? They have? Uhhh. Go **Rams**! What? They have too? O.K. No problem. Go **Seahawks**! (Or whatever you're going to be called.) L.A. has had trouble holding on to major league teams (although to be fair, the Rams did hang around for 30 years) for one simple reason: the **L.A. Memorial Coliseum**. When it was built for the 1932 Olympics it was state of the art. And it even worked for the 1984 Olympics. But it's hard, cold, and badly in need of renovation. The 1994 earthquake didn't help. So now there's talk of building a new facility, possibly near **Dodger Stadium** in Elysian Park, but right now that's all it is—talk. In the meantime, pigskin fans have to be content with the collegiate level, primarily the great **USC** rivalry with **UCLA**. This Pac-10 competition is about more than football, it's a class thing: public school versus private school, brains versus money. Only alumni really care, I suspect. For everyone else it's the point spread that determines who they root for. USC's Trojans play home games at the miserable **L.A. Memorial Coliseum and Sports Arena** (tel 213/740–4672; 3939 S. Figueroa St., Los Angeles), while the Bruins of UCLA have to trek over to Pasadena's **Rose Bowl** (tel 310/825–2101; 991 Rosemont Ave., Pasadena) for their home stands.

Peanuts and Cracker Jack... O.K., now we can get serious. No matter how much Tommy Lasorda may grate on your nerves, there is nothing like a warm summer evening game at **Dodger Stadium** (tel 213/224-1400; Dodger Stadium, 1000 Elysian Park Ave., Elysian Park.) This is a beautiful park with natural grass and palm trees right beyond the outfield wall. Outside the stadium in

Chavez Ravine lies a huge, treelined, picnic-inducing patch of rolling greenery. And even though Lasorda and his splutterings about bleeding Dodger blue are destined to be with us for a while, the team continues to hold surprises. Take last season's sensation, Hideo Nomo, the Japanese pitcher with the impossibly contorted windup. All by himself, Nomo can make you feel good about rooting for the Dodgers and think about buying a new beach ball to take to their next home stand. Even if they lose, a trip to this wonderful stadium is money well spent. If sitting in your car during the bumper-to-bumper parking-lot exodus drives you crazy, I'd suggest parking outside and hiking in. It's all downhill going back.

Hoop dreams... L.A. has two professional basketball teams and even though they've had an uneven 1995–96 season, the **Los Angeles Lakers** are still the team to see. No, most people can't afford the tickets, and with Magic Johnson in and out of retirement, you can bet the scalpers are having a field day. They play at the **Great Western Forum** (tel 310/419–3100; 3900 Manchester Blvd., Inglewood), which has some terrible sight lines unless you're willing to spend a month's rent for tickets. You can get much better seats for much less money and a far more frustrating game by going downtown to see the **Los Angeles Clippers** at the **L.A. Sports Arena** (tel 213/748–6131; 3939 S. Figueroa St.), who every now and then manage to surprise both their disgusted fans and their complacent opponents. Still, they routinely finish in the cellar, so don't expect much.

Slap shots... Just like many politicians, L.A. knows how to build public interest—buy a superstar for your team. Hence the arrival in 1988 of Wayne Gretzky as resident star for the **Los Angeles Kings** (tel 310/480–3282; Great Western Forum, 3900 Manchester Blvd., Inglewood). But money talks, and the Great One walks. He's gone now, and the team is into their rebuilding stage. Basically, that means they've gone from bad to worse, and there's little hope for the future right now. The fan base, however, remains remarkably strong.

The ponies... Although it's not known for its night racing, **Hollywood Park** (tel 310/419–1500; 1050 S. Prairie

Ave., Inglewood) does offer evening opportunities to put down a $2 bet on thoroughbreds. On Friday nights, April through July and November through December, I'll be at the track, thank you. It's only $6 to get in for nine races a night. In between there are simulcasts from other tracks.

Blood sports... For a while it looked like the historic **Grand Olympic Auditorium** (tel 213/749–5171; 1801 S. Grand Ave., downtown L.A.) would bite the dust, smothered by neglect. Built in the twenties for the 1932 Olympics, it was on the ropes, literally. But two years ago it went through a massive renovation which included new seats, lights, and plumbing. These days, this 7,300-seat center for the pugilistic arts is back in business—even though most of the auditorium's money now rolls in from rock concerts. If you want to see boxing, world-class kickboxing, wrestling, or even Roller Derby or sumo, this is the source. Boxing is held on the third Thursday of every month, kickboxing every other month, Roller Derby in the summer. Prices are not cheap, especially for ringside seats, which range from $15 to $75, depending on the event.

Where to play

Batting cages... So you think you're tough? Let's see you climb into the box and face the Koufax machine at the **Glendale Batting Cage** (tel 818/243–2363; 620 E. Colorado St., Glendale). The balls come out of the slot at 82mph. They also have fast- and slow-pitch softball machines here and professional instruction if you need work on your swing. It costs $3.50 for about five minutes, $19.50 for an hour, and will leave you dripping. It's open until 10pm. Over on the west side, check out **Slamo Baseball Batting Cages** (tel 310/398–5050; 5750 Mesmer Ave. behind the Sav-On Drugstore on Jefferson, Culver City). They're also open until 10pm and offer a range of both ball types and ball speeds.

Biking... Do you have *no fear*? For gearheads of both persuasions who have adequate lights, **night biking** offers a totally different experience. Road weenies can muscle up in their big ring to the top of **Griffith Park** via roads that are closed to traffic. Start at the closed-off gate of the park's landscaping facility (at the dead end of Commonwealth Ave., north of Los Feliz Blvd., Los Feliz), and keep bearing to the right. This will take you up to the top of the mountain where the road to the outdoor transportation museum **Travel Town** intersects—about 40 minutes of fairly easy but consistent uphill. You can either turn around here or come down past the observatory and return via the Greek Theatre entrance (which is open to traffic until 10pm). Either way it's a blazing downhill. Watch out for fallen branches and earthquake rubble in the road.

For **mountain bikers** there are scores of possibilities, but a favorite nighttime ride is **Brown Mountain** in Altadena. You park at Millard Canyon Campground (at the end of the Chaney Trail off Loma Alta Drive, Altadena). The trail starts to the left, goes past the bathrooms (where you should fill your water bottles) and the campgrounds, and crosses the creek. From here you bear to your right all the way to the top, about two hours of moderate climbing. Coming back, it's less than 30 minutes of great downhill. The route consists entirely of fire road, with lots of blind curves, so watch for bikers coming up on your descent. Also watch out for mountain lions, which are spotted fairly regularly in this area of the San Gabriels. If you encounter a lion, stay calm and stay with your bike while you retreat—size intimidates the cats. The access road to the campgrounds (where you parked) closes at 10pm, so give yourself time to drive out.

Rack 'em up... Want to see where the yups of the moment rack their balls? It's at the **Westside Billiards Cafe** (tel 310/289–2626; 8612 Beverly Blvd., next to the Hard Rock Cafe at the Beverly Center, Beverly Hills). Pricey food, well-maintained tables, even-better-maintained clientele. Open until 2am, Monday to Saturday, until midnight on Sunday. In WeHo, at **Dome Billiards Cafe** (tel 213/650–1886; 7901 Santa Monica Blvd., at Fairfax, West Hollywood), it's significantly more mainstream and hence more crowded. Good food, a decent bar, and a nice view of the action outside from this second-floor facility. Open until 2am. If you insist on a cold beer with your game of nine-ball, look into Santa

Monica's **Gotham Hall** or the **Hollywood Athletic Club** on Sunset (see The Bar Scene).

Bowling... When the going gets tough, the tough go bowling. And if it's late, they go to **Hollywood Star Lanes** (tel 213/665–4111; 5227 Santa Monica Blvd., Los Angeles). It has 32 lanes and stays open 24 hours. It may not be the cleanest or most high-tech, but where else will you see celebrity-autographed pins? ("Best regards from a real pinhead," wrote Jamie Lee Curtis.) **All Star Lanes** (tel 213/254–2579; 4459 Eagle Rock Blvd., Eagle Rock) is where bowlers on a budget go to strike and spare. They close at midnight, but at $8 an hour (not per game), the 22 lanes are pretty consistently busy. There's a full bar and even a disco area for nonpinheads in the party. Friday nights, local Asian and Latino kids flock to hang out. Finally, another 24-hour site is **Shatto 39 Lanes** (tel 213/385–9475; 3255 W. 4th St., at Vermont, Los Angeles). They have pool tables, a video arcade, a full bar, and, as you might expect, 39 lanes.

Grunion fishing... It's not fishing, exactly—more like catching. These six-inch fish spawn on Southland beaches in spring and summer, during three or four nights following the highest tide after a full moon, usually around midnight. For a couple of hours they wash up on the beach with the waves, bury eggs or shoot sperm, and then, like clubgoers everywhere, try to get back home before the magic wears off. You have to use your bare hands (no nets or pails allowed), and when you panfry them, please offer up a prayer for the unborn. Bring a flashlight and something to carry your catch in. Look in local papers or tackle stores for predictions of when the next run is expected. The best beaches (from Santa Barbara to San Diego) have fine sand, slope gently, and are not crowded with human voyeurs.

Golf... If you want to play nighttime golf, you'll have to go out to **Alhambra Griffith Park Golf Range** (tel 213/663–2555; 4730 Crystal Springs Dr., Griffith Park). You won't get to walk, but you'll get to drive at this quiet, well-lit, double-tiered golf range next to the Wilson/Harding Municipal Golf Course. Lights go off at 11pm, ball machines close at 10:30, and it's $3.50 for a bucket o' balls. There are 29 uncovered stalls and 22 covered on the double-decked platform. The best shot is one that hits the large cutout of a man standing about 200 yards away. When he gets bopped he lets out a mechanical groan. Very satisfying. Also consider the range at **Studio City Golf** (tel 213/877–3777; 4141 Whittsett Ave., two blocks north of Ventura Blvd., Studio City). It's open until 11pm, has 20 stalls, and charges between $3 and $8.50 for a bucket of balls.

For gym rats... Twenty-four-hour gyms are all the rage now, but unfortunately you usually have to be a member. You can check out some, like **Beverly Hills Health & Fitness** (tel 213/658–6999; 8301 Beverly Blvd., Los Angeles) where it costs $10 for a onetime visit. After that, they want you to sign on the dotted line. It's a great gym, however, so if you're only looking for a one-night stand, then give it a try. Free weights, Lifecycles, saunas, tanning beds—pretty much the perfect place to do your L.A. makeover. Once. Which is why I like the **Ketchum Downtown YMCA**. (tel 213/624–2348; 401 S. Hope St., downtown L.A.). It's only $10 to use the facility after 7:30pm and they're open until 10. Saunas, steam rooms, free weights, tons of various Nautilus equipment, and so clean and high-tech you'll think you were in Sly's private gym. This is the gym for the lawyers and financiers who work downtown. In Hollywood, there's the **Hollywood YMCA** (tel 213/467–4161; 1553 Schrader Blvd., Hollywood). The neighborhood leaves a little to be desired, but the facility just had a massive renovation. Open until 9:30pm. All three gyms have racquetball and basketball courts, with great, frenetic pickup games.

Night dives... No, we're not talking about bars. It's an entirely different experience to go scuba diving at night. For one thing, there are all those lobsters you can pick up—as long as it's between September and March. From May through September, the attraction is primarily aesthetic, the water filled with bioluminescent plankton that drift like a curtain around you. Two nearby night dive spots (which you can reach from the beach, without a boat) are in Malibu off Big Rock and off Palos Verdes around Abalone Cove. Come by **Scuba Haus** (tel 310/828–2916; 2501 Wilshire Blvd., Santa Monica) to inquire about equipment rentals (about $50 for everything) and maps to the reefs closest to shore. Scuba Haus is open until 7pm in the summer, 6pm the rest of the year.

Roller skating... For the last 15 years, **World On Wheels** (tel 213/933–5170; 4645½ Venice Blvd., Venice) has been the roller rink of choice for wheel freaks. Kids, teens on dates, families, homies, gangbangers—everybody comes and manages to get along. The music is great, themed for various nights, from oldies to gospel. During the summer, they have all-night skate parties for kids. They lock the doors and don't let them out until the next morning. The **Moonlight Rollerway** (tel 818/241–3630; 5110 San Fernando Rd., Glendale) is a similarly kid-friendly spot. They're open until midnight on the weekends and have *live* organ music.

Shiatsu... So maybe you should have warmed up before you hit the batting cages. Well, thank god for the **Sanwa Health Spa** (tel 213/687–4597; New Otani Hotel, 4th floor, 120 S. Los Angeles St., Little Tokyo). They have a dry sauna ($10), a private Jacuzzi for couples ($25), and shiatsu massage ($48 for 45 minutes, $60 for an hour). You can also get a Swedish massage, but why would you? Open to the public until 11pm but a reservation for a massage is suggested.

Surf casting... True, the Southland has miles of beaches. But unless the grunion are running, usually the only fish you'll see around Santa Monica Bay are those washed up on the sand, killed by some horrible runoff deposited miles away by inland storm drains. You'll see people fishing nonstop off **Santa Monica Municipal Pier** (at the west end of Colorado Avenue, at Ocean Avenue, Santa Monica), but this Southlander sure wouldn't eat anything caught in these waters. A better bet is to head about 10 miles up the coast, to the cleaner waters between **Will Rogers State Beach** and **Malibu Lagoon State Beach**. Basically, the further out of the city you go, the better your luck will be. Supposedly you can land everything from California halibut to white sea bass, but more likely it'll be bonito, mackerel, or rockfish (probably sculpin). Spring and fall are the best seasons, followed by winter, then summer. Plan to lose lots of sinkers.

Swimming... It may not be as architecturally stunning as your local yup gym's lapapoolooza, but the **Echo Park Indoor Pool** (tel 213/481–2640; 1419 Colton St., Echo Park) is enclosed, public, cheap, and usually uncrowded. It's 25 meters long and costs only $1.25 a visit. Adults get the lanes free of kids from 7 to 9pm.

Tennis... If ever there were a sport ideal for L.A. balmy nighttime weather, it's tennis. **The Tennis Place** (tel 213/931–1715; 5880 W. 3rd St., between La Brea and Fairfax, Los Angeles) has everything you need for an evening of torn ligaments: a pro shop, locker room, 16 lighted courts, ball machines, restringing services, and a cafe where you can complain about your partner. It's $13 an hour for nonprime time (before 4pm), $15 for prime, and they're open until 11pm every night; if you want to get a court during the weekend, reserve a week in advance. On the east side, there's **Hillhurst Tennis Center** (tel 213/661–2769; 1600 Hillhurst Ave., Los Feliz). It only has one court and the hours vary, so call ahead. Out in Santa Monica, the public **Lincoln Park** (tel 310/394–6011; 1133 7th St., Santa Monica) has six courts that stay lighted until midnight seven days a week; the fee is $2 per hour a person. Call ahead for reservations.

Trail walking... For the best view of the city at night, head up to the **Griffith Park Observatory** parking lot. Instead of joining the throngs going over to pose next to the James Dean bust, turn east toward the mountains. The trail head begins there and leads up to the top of **Mount Hollywood**. It's free, it's wild, and within a few minutes you'll forget where you are. From here the city is spread out in a 180-degree panorama, framed by pines, and scented by sage and night-blooming jasmine. If you walk all the way to the top it'll take about an hour (bring a flashlight). The trail is fire-road wide and gentle in elevation. The access roads into the park close at 10:30pm, so plan on getting back to your car by 10.

Virtual aerobics... Your first impression of **Virtual World** (tel 818/577–9896; 1 Colorado Ave., Old Town, Pasadena) might be that it's just for kids, an over-the-top video arcade. After all, the lounge menu features peanut-butter-and-jelly sandwiches as an entrée. But face it, kids couldn't afford it. It's Indiana Jones meets Robotech, a total-environment experience where the technician who introduces the system to you wears a tag on his lab coat that reads "Deadman" and there are Martian dinosaur relics in the Virtual Geographic League library. It's not cheap, running about $1 a minute for the slam-bang shoot-'em-up sequences in the pods, which may explain why the place is jammed at lunchtime as business types come in for some tension-venting virtual aerobics. It's lots of fun blowing your buddies to pieces, but it's very popular so call ahead.

Yoga... So you may not break into a sweat, but starting off your evening with some essential stretches will make you much looser than that double martini will. Classes are usually held early, last about 90 minutes, and rates depend on what your interest level is. The **Sivanada Yoga Vedanta Center** (tel 310/822–9642; 1746 Abbot Kinney Blvd., Venice) has open classes weekdays at 7pm. The Tuesday, Wednesday, and Thursday classes are suited to all experience levels and last an hour and a half; on Monday and Friday, more advanced classes last two hours. The **Center For Yoga** (tel 213/464–1276; 230½ N. Larchmont Blvd. between Beverly and 1st, Los Angeles) teaches a variety of styles, including hatha and ashtanga yoga, and welcomes drop-ins. Their latest class is on Wednesdays at 7:30pm, the rest of the week at 7:15. Finally there's **Forrest Yoga Circle** (tel 310/453–5252; 1612 Montana Ave., 2nd floor behind the 17th Street Cafe, Santa Monica), which specializes in ashtanga yoga. There are limited class sizes, the last classes start at 7:30pm, and newcomers are welcome. **B.K.S. Yoga Iyengar Institute** (tel 213/653–0357; 8233 W. 3rd St., Los Angeles) teaches a specialized style of yoga which focuses on body alignment and meditation. A single class is $11 and their latest classes (beginning at 7:30pm) are at the introductory level.

LOS ANGELES & SPORTS

hangi

5

ng out

Say what you want about
the ostentations of
Angelenos; these folks
make for great people
watching. Where else in
the world do men wear
nothing but tennis shorts,

sneakers, and sunglasses in indoor shopping malls? Forget that absurd myth about L.A. being a city where no one walks, and strolling pedestrians are regarded with suspicion by the local constabulary. (It's true that private security forces like Westec, known locally as rent-a-cops, are likely to interrogate you on a street corner if they catch you after dark in Brentwood or Bel Air. But who wants to hang out in well-groomed bastions of the nouveaux riches like that anyway? Also true is the rumor that the L.A.P.D. likes to write jay-walking tickets, particularly in youthquake zones like Westwood, but if you say you're from out of town and plead ignorance, you might dodge the fine.)

Fact is, Angelenos already spend so much time in their cars just getting to work and back that the opportunity to amble aimlessly is cherished. Die-hard Angeleno boosters admit to envying their New York friends who can just walk out the door, turn in any direction, and roam through a world of butcher shops, import boutiques, art galleries, you name it. Here it's a little more complicated but—*emphatically*—not impossible. You have to decide what you're lusting after, then drive, park, and let your mind go. You let the moment create itself, free of hype or any flavor-of-the-month buzz. You are an independent agent, sort of an urban Thoreau, taking time to sniff the exhaust and see the Big Picture. Pasadena's **Old Town** and Santa Monica's **Third Street Promenade** offer pleasant window-shopping, book browsing, and at times an echo of European boulevardier culture. **Melrose Boulevard** hasn't been the same since punk hit in the late seventies. It's calmer now, but has many one-of-a-kind stores and good restaurants. If hoards of testosterone-crazed youth mingling with freakish old-school Los Angeles gutter life are more your style, try **Hollywood Boulevard** or the **Sunset Strip**. Near the UCLA campus, **Westwood** is a scary and always crowded warren of stores and restaurants, most noteworthy to outsiders for its prize collection of movie theaters. These cinemas are outfitted with some of the biggest screens and best sound systems in the world. If you want state-of-the-art, Lucas-inspired screening technology come here. Just because you don't have an agenda—a place to be, a friend to meet, something to do—doesn't necessarily make you a total loser. Really. Sometimes you just want to hang out and observe the passing scene. So, take your pick: These cities-within-a-city are where the hordes of people with *something to do* congregate in depressing numbers. Join them if you will.

The Lowdown

Best window-shopping... **Melrose** is the avenue you could walk for hours and never get farther than a few blocks. You'll be teased constantly with clothes you can't fit into, gadgets you don't need, a lifestyle you don't understand. Park anywhere around La Brea and walk west for as long as you want, maybe to Crescent Heights. Then turn around. Unfortunately, not much is open after 9pm (unless it's close to Christmas or the middle of summer). It doesn't matter. Melrose has the best window displays in the city. And if you're really energetic, then walk down **La Brea** south of Melrose Avenue, towards Wilshire. There are plenty of nice home-furnishing stores down here, mostly on the east side of the street, that will give you an idea of what you could put in your apartment if only the rent weren't so high. **Old Town** in Pasadena (Colorado Blvd., east of Fair Oaks Ave.) is also a major drool for home-furnishings window-shopping. And there are other people on the street doing the same thing as you. Everything is concentrated in a few blocks here, with lots of late-night choices for resting your dogs: coffeehouses, late-night restaurants, and bistros. Even some of the larger chain retail outlets stay open late. It's sort of a grown-up's version of Westwood. Which segues into the real thing: **Westwood** (on and around Westwood Blvd., north of Wilshire). This is probably the most intense window-shopping experience in L.A., with loads of people on the sidewalks late, *and* displays featuring a ton of choice possessions you don't yet have. Parking is a bitch, and the crowds are a bummer, especially in the summer. I avoid it whenever possible, but for college kids with their pockets stuffed with disposable income, it's heaven on earth. Record stores here are open late, and there's a fair amount of street-side activity (vendors and buskers) that keeps things interesting. Finally, there's the **Third Street**

Promenade (3rd St., between Wilshire and Colorado, in Santa Monica), which gets high ratings for the fact that it is the only true walk 'n' shop street in L.A. Instead of going for minimalls on every corner, like the rest of L.A., Santa Monica plopped everything all together. Big crowds, lots of eateries open late, good bookstores, cheap espresso stands, a decent newsstand, and the best people watching in the city (thanks to the very convenient benches). Chaotic but hypnotic, it's "skid row by the sea"; and I love that mix of money and mange. If I didn't live on the east side, I'm sure I'd be a regular here.

Tattoo you... You've just come out of a bar feeling kind of depressed, lonely, without that old joie de vivre. What you need is a tattoo! For impetuous body manipulators, there are plenty of choices. **Spotlight Tattoo** (tel 213/871–1084; 5859 Melrose Ave., Los Angeles; open until 11pm Mon–Sat) is a little removed from the retail madness of Melrose, but the work is totally of the moment. The specialty here is large-format images, Japanese and tribal patterns in particular. Celebs who feel the need for a make-over have traditionally gone to **Sunset Strip Tattoo** (tel 213/650–6530; 8418 Sunset Blvd., West Hollywood; open until midnight). For a sample of their work, check out Axl Rose. As you might expect, they're overpriced and overrated. A relative newcomer to the scene, **Tattoo Mania** (tel 310/657–8282; 8861 Sunset Blvd., West Hollywood; open until 3am weekends, 11pm Sun–Mon, 1am Tue–Thur) has quickly established itself as less trendoid, but the place to come if it's way late. Popular with bikers—not just-bought-a-Harley-cuz-of-midlife-crisis bikers, but *real* bikers.

The marriage of tattoo parlor and art gallery was an idea whose time had come, and **Purple Panther Design** (tel 213/882–8165; 7560 Sunset Blvd., Hollywood) pulls it off by attracting both modern primitives and gallery hoppers. Other skin-changer shops stay open late, but this is the only one where you can buy a framed print of a design and live with it on your wall before you decide to die with it on your body.

Antiques and objets after dark... On the second Friday of every month, look for **Chasse de La Brea** (tel 714/631–3232; at the corner of 6th St. and S. La Brea, one block north of Wilshire). This is a new outdoor venture that brings together a wide variety of dealers selling a wild assortment of goods: art, furniture, estate jewelry, clothing, rugs, toys. It's open until 11pm on Fridays and winds up the next day at 6pm. Think of those outdoor markets that work so well in lower Manhattan and you'll get the idea—except this is catered by La Brea Bakery, has valet service, and delivers. Stumbling across the cozy little **Off the Beaten Track** (tel 213/935–8541; 5859 W. 3rd St., Los Angeles) may be the best surprise of the night. Usually open until midnight, it's unassuming, friendly, and totally true to its name, offering unusual art and refinished furniture. It's the place to go if you want that old desk to get a decoupage treatment and, at the same time, get into an educated discussion with people who love their work. It may look like a junk store from the street, but go inside and you'll be amazed. More than once I've found myself rearranging my living room in the middle of the night only to realize that what I need is a perfect, little end table to put my old magazines on. That's the time for a trip down Melrose to the city's only 24-hour furniture shop, **Burke's Country Pine** (tel 213/655–1114; 8080 Melrose Ave., Hollywood). You can't miss the place simply because the furniture is out on the sidewalk, brightly lit, all day, all night. They sell tables, headboards, dressers, chairs, and bureaus.

Browsing for books... When it's late, and you want to read something but just don't know what, head for **Book Soup** (tel 310/659–3110; 8818 Sunset Blvd., West Hollywood). Packed floor to ceiling with new fiction and nonfiction, an extensive back list, art books, collectors items, one-of-a-kind finds, and signed copies. My favorite bookstore on either coast. If you're on the west side and looking for something rare and used (like that mint first-edition copy of *Jonathan Livingston Seagull*), check out **The Novel** (tel 310/396–8566; 212 Pier Ave., Santa Monica). It's part coffeehouse, part bookstore, but it feels mostly like a post-Apocalypse library. Books are stacked high on two levels, and a sign warns browsers that the place is guarded by Wei D'To, "Protector of books against fire, pillaging, decay, and dishonest borrowers." Open until 1am. The best-smelling bookstore in L.A. has to be **The Daily Planet** (tel 213/957–0061; 5931½ Franklin Ave., Hollywood). There's a heady selection of scented candles, incense, soaps, and aroma-therapy goods on sale. While the book selection is limited, it's well thought out, offering some of the most interesting titles in many left-brain genres: modern Japanese literature, lesbian erotica, Beat Generation ravings, and those of Generation X. In ten minutes I found three books I had to have. Open until midnight.

Browsing for newspapers and magazines... For years it seemed that the **World Book & News** newsstand (tel 213/465–4352; 1652 N. Cahuenga Blvd., Hollywood) was the *only* newsstand of note in the city. It's got lots of competitors now, but still leads the pack for being open 24 hours and for getting in new magazines days (and sometimes weeks) before other places. They also have an impressive selection of hometown papers, computer titles, industry trades, and reference books. **Centerfold International Newsstand** (tel 213/651–4822; 716 N. Fairfax Ave., Hollywood), as the name implies, is where you come when you're looking for that Ukranian weekly newspaper your grandmother used to read. Noted for employing Hollywood underground musicians, Centerfold stays open until midnight and in addition to your standard mix probably has more Eastern European papers, magazines, and expat journals than any other newsstand.

Browsing for adult toys... Just about every X-rated bookstore has some sexual accessories for sale, but to really grasp the range of possibilities, come by **The Pleasure Chest** (tel 213/650–1022; 7733 Santa Monica Blvd., West Hollywood). Totally delightful in its crassness and blasé willingness to offer anything two (or more) consenting adults might be willing to do to their own (or another's) body, this is kind of a cross between Victoria's Secret and The Sharper Image. Open until 1am, it's a West Hollywood landmark, another indication that we're not in Kansas anymore. The clientele is straight, gay, coed, and the mood is playful and humorous, with none of the wheezing furtiveness found in adult bookstores. Further west, at the corner of Santa Monica and La Cienega, you'll find **Drake's** (tel 310/289–8932; 8932 Santa Monica Blvd., West Hollywood). A higher-end stop with pleasant, bright lighting, Drake's gets visits from sedate couples out on a lark—who can resist the discreet charm of sexual self-help shops?—and it also has a stronger emphasis on gay and lesbian accessories and diversions. Right in the heart of the gay 'n' play nightlife section of West Hollywood, this is the last stop before going home. They're open until 2:30am; and when I came in they had an "Absolutely Fabulous" episode playing on the monitor, which was good enough reason to hang around. Up in Hollywood, **Casanova's Adult World** (tel 213/848–9244; 7766 Santa Monica Blvd., Hollywood) has magazines, videos, toys, and even CD-ROMs; it stays open until 2 am. If it gets really late, the only place to go for around-the-clock toy shopping is **Le Sex Shoppe** (tel 213/464–9435; 6315½ Hollywood Blvd., Hollywood). It's also in Hollywood, which means the neighborhood and clientele are both slightly gamier than in West Hollywood. This is one of a chain of five adult stores; and if you can't find what you need here, then you probably already have it.

To the baths... Quintessentially Californian, the pinnacle of Me Decade hedonism, relics of another era, hot tub clubs are a special place to whiddle away those restless late-night hours. A so-called relaxation spa that stays open until 4am, **Splash** has two outlets, one in West Hollywood, one in Santa Monica (tel 213/653–4410, 8054 W. 3rd. St., at Crescent Heights, West Hollywood; tel 310/479–4657, 10932 Santa Monica Blvd., Santa Monica). Since the AIDS epidemic has shut down so many baths, Splash is one of the few private facilities still catering to those who like to get really, really clean. The clientele is mixed—men, women, gay, straight—and the 18 rooms are private. It's the kind of place couples go early in the evening to celebrate their 20th anniversary. Start with your basic whirlpool ($15 an hour per person) and graduate to the extravagent, soap-opera-inspired heights of over-size Jacuzzi rooms with cable TV, VCR, waterfall, aquarium, bidet, wet bar, and more ($50 an hour per person). And it *is* clean, with the water chlorinated and continuously filtered, and all surfaces in the room disinfected after each use. They're licensed by the L.A. County Health Board.

For cigar chompers... Slapping a big stogie in your mug is no longer just for the tough guys. It's a yup thing now. Not only does it make you appear manly, but also taller. Look at Sly and Arnold. A new breed of cigar shops now sponsor smoke nights, strange men's-club rituals where groups of aficionados mingle and puff themselves comatose. **Up in Smoke** (tel 213/654–8173; 8278 Santa Monica Blvd., West Hollywood), a little storefront down from Theater Row, has smoke-ins on Sunday evenings, and is open for purchases until 11 on the weekends, 10 the rest of the week. **Phillip Dane's Cigar Lounge** (tel 310/285–9945; 9669 S. Santa Monica Blvd., on Little Santa Monica between Bedford and Roxbury, Beverly Hills) takes the noxious weed to a whole nother level. They carry 60 premium brands, have all kinds of accessories for the true ash-head, and are open until midnight or until the last ash drops. People will never glare at you here for lighting up. For my money, the absolute hippest joint to light up is at **Bloom's General Store** (tel 213/687–6571; 714 Traction St., downtown; open until 11:30 weekends, 11 weekdays), where you can find some of the best hand-wrappeds in all of the east side. Bloom's hosts cigar nights on Tuesdays, starting at 8.

Groceries after hours… There are lots of supermarkets that are open until midnight or later, but the WeHo **Pavilion's** (tel 310/273–0977; 8969 Santa Monica Blvd., West Hollywood) is a special case. Known to locals as "the gay Pavilion's," you come here to stock up on your weekly needs and do a little cruising at the same time. It's yupscale in tone and offers an amazing selection of gourmet foods and incredibly fresh produce. It's perfect for last-minute birthday shopping for home chefs. Open 24 hours. If you're looking for specialty items like deli food, wines, or smoked fish, there's always **Greenblatt's** (tel 213/656–0606, 8017 Sunset Blvd., Hollywood; open until 2am). They've been around longer than you've been alive probably. Very clean, great variety, and the deli items are not all greasy and overcooked. This is where Hollywood-area celebs send their gofers for a take-out nosh.

Late-night electronics and film… Where do all the insomniac geeks go for a techno fix? **The Good Guys** (tel 310/659–6500; 100 N. La Cienega Blvd., West Hollywood) is open 24 hours and is about the only place to come when it's 4am and your TV just went out in the middle of that World Cup match coming in live from Rome. The computer section sucks, but the rest of the store is your standard quasi-discount house. It's way late, and the motor drive on your Nikon just ate *the* shot you've been trying to get all night. The closest thing in

L.A. to a photographer's pro shop is **Pix** (tel 213/936–5183; 211 S. La Brea Ave., Hollywood), a professional processing lab and 24-hour source for film and battery needs. If one of the knowledgeable staff members can't unjam your camera, they'll rent you a new one.

Flowers... Ever wanted to turn up at your lover's house at dawn with an enormous bouquet of fresh flowers? Then you've got to head down to the **Flower Market** (on Wall St., between 7th and 8th Sts., downtown). This is the closest it comes to a genuine city-that-never-sleeps experience. Plus, you come out of it smelling wonderfully. The Flower Market is bustling between the hours of 3 and 6am, and the vendors are very agreeable. (Who wouldn't be at this hour?) You can get some real bargains here; and if you don't mind slightly imperfect stems, you can get an armful for pennies on the petal. If you're *really* cheap, try diving in the nearby parking lot dumpsters. Look for petals on the ground next to the bins. They can produce surprising (if extra aromatic) rewards.

Hair styling... You have to make an appointment at **Norm Tuch Hair Co.** (tel 213/655–7535; 8210 W. 3rd St., Los Angeles), but they're willing to hang around until late to do your 'do. But what if you wake up out of a nightmare and realize you have to have a red-tinted buzz cut done before that 9am breakfast meeting? No worries. Head for **Hollywood Hair Designs** (tel 213/464–9938; 6317 Hollywood Blvd., Hollywood), where you can get everything done to your hair, 24 hours a day. It's a terrifying freedom. Use it wisely.

Singles, LPs, and CDs... When a hypnotic dub-jungle mix on the car radio catches your ear, it's good odds you'll find it at either **Tower Records** (tel 310/657–7300; 8801 Sunset Blvd., West Hollywood) or the **Virgin Megastore** (tel 213/650–8666; 8000 Sunset Blvd., Hollywood). They're both massive, but Virgin gets the nod from me for their better selection of world beat, reggae, and imports. I love all those listening posts scattered around the store; plus, there's a **Buzz** coffee house *and* a **Wolfgang Puck Cafe** just outside, in the arcade. Both of these record outlets are open until midnight. But much more interesting to my ears (plus it has a tremendous used CD selection) is **Aron's** (tel 213/469–4700; 1150 N. Highland Ave.,

Hollywood; open until midnight weekends, 10 the rest of the week). It has a great dub section and bins full of rare and unusual indies, both new and used. **Penny Lane** (tel 310/319–5333; 1349B Third St. Promenade, Santa Monica; open until midnight weekends) gets a mention for being the Promenade's weirdest record store, tiny in size but carrying vinyl and non–major label rarities.

Toys, gifts, geegaws... There aren't too many places in the world you can find a windup Godzilla at 11pm. That's why God invented Melrose Avenue. Try **The Soap Plant** (tel 213/651–5587; 7400 Melrose Ave., West Hollywood). They're open late (midnight during the summer) and have just about everything you never knew you wanted: Day of the Dead artifacts, weird cookbooks, skull and punk jewelry, chili-pepper lights, Japanese and Chinese toys, collectors' art books found nowhere else, Haitian voodoo flags, one-of-a-kind masks from all over the world. The list goes on and on. And if it's not here, check next door at its sister store, **Wacko** (tel 213/651–3811; 7416 Melrose Ave., West Hollywood), where the emphasis is on even more toys, dolls, cards, and increasingly useless items. Looking for a souvenir to take home? You'll find it here. If you happen to be out by the beach looking for that "Charlie's Angels" doll that used to grace your bureau 15 years ago, come by **Mayhem** (tel 310/451–7600; 1411 Third St. Promenade, Santa Monica; open until 1am weekends, 11pm weekdays). They've got all sorts of pop-cult trash, the things your parents always said exemplified bad taste.

Women's clothing... I don't know anyone who shops for sweaters late at night. A perfect vinyl skirt to go with those torn fishnets? That's a different concept. Welcome to **Retail Slut** (tel 213/934–1339; 7308 Melrose Ave., Hollywood; open until 11pm on weekends); they've got the Hollywood-trash look down cold. Also consider **Nana Trading Company** (tel 310/394–9690; 1228 Third St. Promenade, Santa Monica; open until 11:30 on weekends) for a slightly more earth-toned, if nonetheless combative look. Nana is where you get Doc Martens, cheap retro jewelry à la Madonna in *Desperately Seeking Susan*, baggy skate-rat clothes, rave sunglasses, and other goodies for the folks back in Peoria.

Best cruising with a killer sound system... First of all: not on my street. Please. Take your ride up to **Hollywood Boulevard** (between Vine St. and La Brea Ave.) on a Friday or Saturday night and idle your way down the boulevard of broken dreams. You'll have plenty of company. Valley kids love this cruise, and have flocked here like lemmings for decades. The police close it off now—or at least set up roadblocks—on many weekends, checking for intoxication and curfew violators. But that's part of the fun. Figure that it'll take you a good hour to get to your turnaround point (Mann's Chinese Theater or the Roosevelt Hotel). You'll be able to ogle desperate streetwalkers, transvestites, homeless people, Scientologists, dazed runaways, deportees from our Reaganized mental hospitals—all from the safety of your 400-watt force field. It's like a terrible accident on the freeway that fascinates and repels at the same time.

Best sunset view from the city... During the summer smog season from July to September, you might not see much, but the rest of the year the view from the **Griffith Park Observatory**'s walkways and balconies (tel 213/664–1181; 2800 E. Observatory Rd., Griffith Park) makes living in the city almost worthwhile. On clear days, you can see all the way from the towers of Century City to the rough hump of Catalina Island, 26 miles off San Pedro. It's free and family friendly.

Best sunset view, period... It's not exactly freeway convenient, but for the drop-dead California sunset that will make the rest of the evening seem like a letdown, take the **Pacific Coast Highway** to **Corral Canyon Road** in Malibu. Take a right and go all the way to the end of the road. You can enjoy the view from here—of the ocean, the coast, the San Fernando Valley—or hike a few hundred feet up to the top of the rocks to your right.

Best sunset walk... For the inner-city prisoner, the illusion of escape is possible at **Pacific Palisades Park** (between Montana and Colorado, on Ocean Ave., Santa Monica). The Palisades are perpetually, inevitably receding, beset by a bad case of geological gingivitis. Every heavy rainstorm or aftershock sends a little bit more down the slope toward the Pacific Coast Highway. But

LOS ANGELES ⟨ HANGING OUT

that's part of L.A.'s ephemeral attraction. Everything—even the earth you're standing on—has a limited shelf life. The Pacific is boundless from here, going all the way to the curvature of the horizon. Turn your back on the traffic and imagine yourself in one of those tiny boats pushing slowly into the sunset. This view is the best reason to live in Santa Monica.

Best walk on the water... It's unfortunate but true: Walking down on the water's edge is not advisable in Santa Monica or Venice. Maybe nothing will happen, or maybe you'll get mugged or raped. The safest stroll is over the water, on the **Santa Monica Municipal Pier** (at the end of Colorado Ave., west of Ocean, Santa Monica). Half honky-tonk, half yupped-up Santa Monica, it's family friendly, salty, well policed, and egalitarian. Am I a Pollyanna for loving the merry-go-round? Late at night, nothing will bring you back to earth faster than watching the waves break over the pilings.

Museums... Museums are not your typical nighttime entertainment, but they should be. Think of them as an alternative to meeting for a drink somewhere. Since they tend to close at 8 or 9, it's just a teaser for the evening. Want to show your date just how sophisticated you are? Say "No, let's not meet at a smoky bar. I'll see you in front of the hair-and-dust sculpture at the Museum of Jurassic Technology." That's class. Definitely *not* class is meeting in front of the Beatles at the **Hollywood Wax Museum** (tel 213/462–8860; 6767 Hollywood Blvd., Hollywood). Sure they're open until 2am on the weekends, but that's the only appeal.

The museum-with-the-mostest will forever be the **Museum of Contemporary Art/Temporary Contemporary** (tel 213/626–6222; 152 N. Central Ave., Little Tokyo), the wayward child of L.A. institutional art. It's open until 8pm on Thursdays and is abiding proof that a museum doesn't have to be stodgy, dull, or only for the dead-animal-pelts-and-pearls set. Since its inception in the 1980s it has done more than any other large institution to give local artists a sense of worth and art lovers in general a communal source of pride. Located on a dead-end street in Little Tokyo in what feels like an old warehouse, it was intended to simply be a temporary space (hence the name) while the more elegant Arata Isozaki–

designed permanent location was being built on Bunker Hill. But the TC just won't die, thank god. And, ironically, it is a vastly superior space to its multimillion-dollar sibling up the hill to the west. Always interesting and challenging, it mixes functionality, anonymity, and irreverence in equal parts. And shows that are just too outré for the main building happily find a home here. Meanwhile, up in the tonier neighborhood of Bunker Hill, is the *real* museum, the **Museum of Contemporary Art (MOCA)** (tel 213/626–6222; 250 S. Grand Ave., at California Plaza, downtown; open until 8pm Thur). After some lengthy prodding by local art critics, the museum is finally starting to exhibit its permanent collection, a frontrunner in Los Angeles and California–based artists. Admittedly, the field has few competitors, but that will change when the new Getty complex finally opens in the Santa Monica mountains. Memorable for its pyramid skylights, the Isozaki-designed Contemporary has a placid, pretty exterior, but the galleries tend to be too constrictive for adventurous exhibitions. That's why the TC exists. MOCA is somehow not as daring as you would want a contemporary art museum to be, but the building itself, perched on a hillside plaza overlooking downtown, deserves a visit.

Moving east, there's the recently-revived grandmother of L.A. museums, the **Los Angeles County Museum of Art** (tel 213/857–6000; 5905 Wilshire Blvd., Mid-Wilshire; open until 9pm Fri). For nearly two years it's been without a director, and the lack of a hand at the helm seems to have been a blessing in disguise. The programs seem to be getting better and better—it's interesting to note that the retrospective of native son and conceptual troublemaker Mike Kelly ended up here instead of at MOCA. In architectural terms, this is what a museum is supposed to look like—at least in our imaginations. It has huge classic spaces, a sense of cultural weight, and the pleasant, faint bouquet of rot emanating from the La Brea Tar Pits, just down the street. It hosts an excellent film series and free concerts as well. Ironically, the museum with the least interesting curating is the newest and most convenient to strolling foot traffic: The **Santa Monica Museum of Art** (tel 310/399–0433; 2437 Main St., Santa Monica; open until 10pm Fri) sits near restaurants and bars on a trendy stretch of Main Street. Large, spartan, and vaguely industrial, the space looks like a tasteful but anonymous gallery. They get points for trying, however, especially when it comes to experimental terrain like Bob Flanagan's celebrations of S&M and pain. Finally, there's the uniquely L.A. **Museum of Jurassic Technology** (tel 310/836–6131; 9341 Venice Blvd., West Los Angeles; open until 8pm Thur). Who knows what it means, but the publicly declared mission of this tiny space is for the "advancement of knowledge and the public appreciation of the Lower Jurassic." Think of a museum created by the B-52's, and you're getting close to the vibe.

Gallery openings as nightlife... Don't ignore the importance of gallery openings when you're looking for a strings-free evening out. Some of the best parties I've ever been to have taken place in the city's galleries, chatting up an interesting blend of strangers, washing down free cheese and crackers with decent wine. Check out the *L.A. Weekly* for gallery openings, and don't worry if you're not on the list—there *is* no list. Gallery-opening hours vary wildly according to the artist, the crowd expected, and the gallery owner's personal finances. For the latest dirt on galleries and artists, look for a copy of the 'zine *Caligula* at your less reputable boho hangs.

Really thirsty culture vultures flock to **Bergamot Station** (2525 Michigan Ave., Santa Monica), a strip mall with art galleries instead of your typical liquor store–Laundromat–convenience store combo. On weekends, you can gallery hop from one opening to another, slurping down white wine while ignoring what's hanging on the walls. Three of the Bergamot Station hot spots are worth dropping by. **Rosamund Felsen** (tel 310/828–8488) is the postmodernists' home away from home, where Mike Kelly peers and clones come to deconstruct life as we know it. The gallery hosts lots of media-based work and generally high-quality art that is fairly priced. In a fairly utilitarian industrial space, **Shoshana Wayne** (tel 310/453–7535) shows interesting young artists; unlike many galleries, she includes women. Shoshana has very intriguing installations and is not afraid to take a chance on an ambitious exhibition that may not make money but will bring in the crowds. Always fun. As the name suggests, the **Gallery of Functional Art** (tel 310/829–6990) is art you use: lamps, furniture, screens, bathroom fixtures. It's more fun than cruising Ikea, but slightly more pricey.

Elsewhere around the city, you should check out Beverly Hills's **Margo Leavin Gallery** (tel 310/273–0603; 812 N. Robertson Blvd., Los Angeles), one of the oldest galleries of its caliber in the city. Situated in an old house that has been totally gutted and rebuilt, it's now a very slick space that highlights blue-chip icons from pop and minimalism. A sprinkling of notable, young up-and-comers occasionally also get the nod. On the west side, there's the venerable **L.A. Louver** (tel 310/822–4955; 45 N. Venice Blvd., Venice), a gallery particularly strong in British artists and California assemblages. It has a lock on the massive collection of Wallace Berman, a famous Southern California collector with wide-ranging taste. The space is new, on three floors, and totally upscale. If you have to ask, you can't afford it.

For the photographic field, the only choice is **G. Ray Hawkins** (tel 310/394–5558; 910 Colorado Ave., Santa Monica), the oldest and most respected photo fine arts dealer in the city. The gallery has everything from vintage to new, and the prices are not that off-putting. Probably the best value in fine art.

Best gallery parties... On the low-rent side of things, there's **Acme** (tel 310/264–5818; 1800B Berkeley St., Santa Monica), which does younger artists, wilder artists, totally weirded-out, never-make-a-dime artists. Great openings, affordable art, no pearls in sight. And don't forget **Dan Bernier** (tel 310/264–4882; 3026½ Nebraska Ave., Santa Monica). Again, there's a young street vibe, great installations, and the sense of seeing work by artists with absolutely nothing to lose. Another major favorite among young conceptualists and playful street urchins with a chip on their palette is **Thomas Solomon's Garage** (tel 213/654–4731; 928 N. Fairfax Ave., Los Angeles). It's funny, unintimidating, and affordable. Finally, on the east side, there's **La Luz de Jesus Gallery** (tel 213/666–7667; at the Soap Plant, 4633 Hollywood Blvd., Los Feliz), which used to be located above the Soap Plant store on Melrose. They're usually way off the wall, so cutting edge you'll want to bring Band-Aids, but they hold the best gallery-opening bashes in the city—maybe on the entire West Coast.

late nigh

t dining

6

You do not survive the
night on music, smoke,
and alcohol alone.
Sometimes you need fuel.
Believe it or not, few cities
in the world can compete
with L.A.'s late-night grub

scene. You can go healthy or greasy, sour or sweet, bland or industrial-strength spicy. Even though nutritionists advise against eating a heavy meal late at night, there's something wonderfully wicked about sitting down to a greasy hunk of beef covered in chili at a time when you should be home safely tucked in bed. Maybe because L.A. is the quintessential car town, it has a better grasp on eating from fast-food stands than even New York. True, you won't find the ubiquitous pizza slice or hot dog vendor on every corner—but who wants that kind of junk when you can eat authentic chili fries smothered in onions and cheese (a dish known as chili fries that is apparently indigenous to the west)? Or a real burrito *with refried beans,* not some charlatan's allegedly healthy nouvelle imitation of San Francisco Mission-style burritos with black beans and spinach. Or bonito fresh from the Pacific? And if you want California nouvelle cuisine, can you think of a better place to try it (O.K., except maybe the Bay Area)? There's no better indication of L.A.'s ethnic mix than the fact that your choices are global, no matter how late it gets. So keep your eye on the road, and let your taste buds do the walking.

The Lowdown

Bagels, who knew?... The most reliably satisfying late-night stop you can make is the **Brooklyn Bagel Bakery**. They're open until 3am on weekends, 11pm the rest of the week, and for the price of a dozen you get 13. That's sesame, onion, garlic, salt, water, egg, raisin, or chips. Plus cream cheese (though easterners should be forewarned they only have plain). If they only sold *The New York Times,* you'd be set.

Latino... Don't let the deconstructionist architecture deter you from resting your dogs in the cafeterialike expanse of the **Gaucho Grill** on Santa Monica's Third Street Promenade. Don't worry; you're not going to get a sprinkling of premature veggies tastefully arranged in a minimalist pattern. It's beef, chicken, empanadas, curly fries, and heavy garlic on everything. A hearty eater's heaven, this place gets raves from both Anglo and Hispanic diners. Vegetarians should sink their teeth into the veggie brochette, stuffed with mushrooms, peppers, eggplant, zucchini, and onions. And if you're dining alone, the Promenade's well-stocked newsstand is right out front with plenty of reading material. No dish costs more than $12.

Desperately seeking celebs... The latest project of chef and scene maker Joachim Splichal is **Pinot Hollywood,** located in the old space of the eighties industry hot spot Columbia Bar & Grill. Convenient to studios (it's right down the street from KTLA), pricey but definitely worth the money, this is the natural habitat for starlets who will order a salad and onion soup but wind up eating all the fries off your plate. The men are likely to have expensive eyewear and Pat Riley–style coiffures. They serve up great steaks, sandwiches, and grilled sausages. It's hard to know just where **Van Go's Ear** belongs on the food chain. This low-key 24-hour eatery in an old wood house on Venice's oh-so-trendy Main Street has sandwiches, teriyaki, wonderful omelettes, protein drinks (including the rather indulgent-sounding "Fruit Fuck"), an art gallery, and, for smokers, an outside balcony overlooking Main. It's popular with beach denizens, upmarket celebs (Madonna, Sonny Bono, Jay Leno, JFK Jr.), and people who just need a comfortable place to figure out where they are before they go home—in short, the kind of place you wish were in your neighborhood.

When in Cali... When I was letting my lightly grilled tuna dissolve in my mouth, I forgot for a moment I was within boom-box distance of the Promenade. More midtown-Manhattan than Cal-chic Santa Monica, **Pentola Taverna** is a restaurant for grown-ups, with polished and stained wood everywhere, generic abstract fabric designs on the walls, huge potted plants, strands of garlic and Santa Fe peppers hanging over the windows. Think civilized yet funky. An excellent wine list goes hand in hand with Asian-accented bistro dishes, like seared *ahi* steaks rolled in pepper. Over at the Pacific Design Center, there's foodie maven Bruce Marder's **fusion at pdc**, where the California brasserie dishes offer a pleasant contrast to the high-tech overload of the decor: You can watch yourself enter the restaurant on scattered video monitors. Playful, friendly, and totally attitude free, this is what mature late-night dining should be like everywhere. Where else could you go from to-die-for borscht to gravlax on walnut toast to pumpkin ravioli to *ahi* tuna with a potato puree? Plus, it's *cheap*! Maybe because it's new or because the restaurant, which sits inside a shopping mall-like showroom, isn't visible from the street, it's easy to get a seat right now.

A touch of rhythm with the jerked chicken... There's no regular closing time at **Little Ricky's** in Old Pasadena. Basically, they stay open until people aren't coming in anymore—maybe until 1:30am on weekends—and usually at that hour you can't find food like this: gourmet Cuban-Mexican dishes cooked only with fresh ingredients, and with zero lard. Once a month there's Cafe Caliente, a Latin theme night which brings in poets, musicians, and artists. The crowd resembles the three owners: young, bicultural, and playful. Want to meet the next Los Lobos or Frank Romero? Drop by Little Ricky's for *papa rellas* (mashed-potato balls stuffed with beef) and a Coco-Rico soda. Also in Pasadena, **La Bamba** manages to bring the tropical flair of the Caribbean to this staid brick and old-money neighborhood. The food is delicious and authentic—particularly the jerked chicken, which mixes spices sour and sweet, and the *lechon asado*, slow-roasted pork with onions. For vegans, try the "Monkey Casserole" and tell them to hold the *picadillo* meat sauce. For everyone—the smooth-as-silk butterscotch flan is worth a visit, even if you're not going to eat anything else. Conga drums hang from pillars, surrounded by strands of colorful ribbon. Live music—Latin jazz, salsa, steel drums—is often featured weekends, and there's a nice dance area near the long wooden bar. La Bamba is also the scene of an impromptu harp-blowing session from a regular street musician named Michael, who frequently stops by. O.K., time to dance off those calories! That's why you come to **El Floridita,** the closest you'll get to Havana in L.A. The lobster, paella, and empanadas are fab, but it's the after-*comida* tango that keeps me. They have great salsa bands six nights a week, and while you're out on the dance floor, look for Robert Duvall—he's a regular. Have a *mojito* (sort of a Cuban mint julep) and get out there and mambo!

Chinese fusion... It's late. Your date is hungry for something Italian, maybe *osso buco* with pesto linguini. You're in the mood for something lighter—maybe moo shu duck with a side of spring rolls. No problem! At **Ciao Yie,** in Pasadena's Old Town, you can both be satisfied. This is L.A.'s only Chinese-Italian restaurant, an East-West marriage that seamlessly blends both cuisines. Owner Chao Yeh lived in Italy for 20 years, and does the cross-cultural dance with great subtlety. Tasteful and light in delivery, this is the perfect late-night food. If you're not sure what to try, check out their grazing specialties which come in dim sum–sized portions. More generic in style, but open later than Ciao Yie, is **Yangtze**, on the Third Street Promenade. They try to cover the bases of the Pacific Rim, melding Chinese, Thai, and Japanese entrées—with limited success. The sushi is half price if you sit at the bar, but the decor inside is so horribly low-rent Frank Gehry, with off-kilter wall angles straight out of the eighties, that it may be a better value to sit outside on the Promenade and watch the human parade.

Over easy, and a cuppa joe?... When the aliens land their spaceships in L.A., you can bet they'll go for a late-night snack at one of the all-night, Jetsons-era coffee shops that litter the landscape, restaurant remainders from the bygone Tomorrowland futurism of the fifties. At all of these dreams-of-days-past stick to breakfast, endless coffee, or a burger. Anything else is taking your life in your hands. **Norm's** is the place to begin. Perched neatly at the side of the Santa Monica Freeway, it's your basic all-night coffee shop. The food is way better than its chain-feed neighbor Denny's, prices are cheap (at last check steak and eggs were under $10), and it's ambience free. Yes, Norm's is startlingly normal, as the coffeehouse at the start of the Trans America Highway should be. The queen of the night is still **Ships,** home of the Ship Shape burger, endless coffee, white-bread sandwiches, and waitresses frozen in amber. It doesn't get any more Jetsons spaceage futurama than this. The Ship Shape burger, which despite its name is just a burger, is just what you need late at night (or early in the morning). For my money, the Sunset Strip begins and ends at one point: **Ben Frank's**. They're trying to stay current by adding dishes like salmon with dill and lobster stir-fry, but face it, this is a coffee shop. You want a burger, meat loaf, fries, a milk shake? The workers of the night—musicians, strippers, streetwalkers, cops—all come here because it's always open. They serve champagne, although if you don't like cold duck, don't chance it. Studio musicians taking a short break hold their noises and drop by the Rock and Roll Denny's. That's not the real name, of course. It's a **Denny's** just like the rest of 'em, but maybe because ageless deejay of L.A.'s ur-alternative station KROQ, Rodney Binginheimer, used to practically live here, it's marginally hip. The food is no better than any other Denny's. It's totally lacking in ambience and the chow isn't as cheap as it should be, but it's freeway-close on the Sunset Strip. This is a no-other-alternative choice. The coffee's lousy, the food tastes like cardboard–only the antics of the club kids in the booth behind you make this worth a visit.

Old New York delis à la SoCal... Now that Ziggy's is gone, only **Canter's** is left for a 4am pastrami on rye. For years this was punk central, and more than a few food fights have taken place under the disapproving steely eyes of the babushka waitresses. Eat all your food! Whatsamatta? The pastries are tired and heavy, the pastrami dry rather than greasy. Overall, it's a meal that will still be with you the next night. I've learned to just have iced tea, but you should still drop by because it's still a scene. Before the hangover sets in, this is where you come to try to recoup. You haven't done late-night until you've done Canter's. Much more continental in tone and less of a scene is **Operetta**. Light pastries are kneaded before your eyes; excellent, lean and mean deli meats and salads are served, and the food is full on the tongue but light on the heart. I found it by accident, cruising down Third after everything else had closed. People sit out front, nursing espressos, or shop for late-next-morning brunch supplies. Where else can you get a fluffy tiramisu at this time of the morning?

Something's fishy... Santa Monica is your hands-down choice for fast fish late at night. Way up the Pacific Coast Highway, the **Reel Inn** is a swimmingly good seafood restaurant in the L.A. area—my favorite, in fact, during normal hours. Now, thanks to the new Third Street Promenade outlet, you don't have to trek to Malibu anymore. This is the place to come for totally fresh fish, honestly presented, without any hoopla, heavy sauces, or high-tech overkill; the menu offers special catch-o'-the-day dishes. Basic, real, and wonderful. I've never had a meal here I wouldn't have again. The ambience is cafeterialike, but who cares? This is great fish at an everyman's price. For greasy fish and chips, there's really nothing better than **Ye Olde King's Head,** also in Santa Monica. This is the best pub in L.A. (see The Bar Scene), but it deserves a double mention for the crisp, vinegary blend of this most basic Brit fast food, along with the trad bangers 'n mash and spud-loaded shepherd's pie. The ambience is over-the-top, but the place is large enough to allow an easy retreat, though you should brace yourself for slow-as-molasses service.

Grease pits... Don't feel guilty for reading this. According to the By Night Research & Biking Foundation, grease is one of the three essential food groups of Late Night Nutrition—the other two being alcohol and caffeine. So, naturally we begin with french-fried potatoes: **Benita's Fries,** a small storefront on the Third Street Promenade which serves only fries—nothing else. Small serving or large, one sauce or two. That's it. For less than $5 you'll be in spud paradise. Not exactly in harmony with the tight-jeans body-con environment of WeHo, **Hamburger Haven** manages to survive by living up to its advertising: The best burgers in town. Sounds like a wild claim, but the simple "Naked Burger" (just dressing and pickle) could be included in most burger-lovers' all-time top ten. The semienclosed patio is smack dab in middle of the West Hollywood gay play zone. On Beverly Boulevard near Rampart there's **Tommy's,** home of the messiest beef 'n' beans package ever served up in a wrapper. You'll see various Tommy's rip-offs as you cruise the city, but don't be fooled. This is the one— the original, the world-famous, the notorious. Comfortably close to the police station in an area know as the Ramparts, it's crawling late at night with people who need a big dose of grease ASAP! The burgers are served up assembly-line style, dipped in chili, draped in onions—messy as open-heart surgery. This is another late-night rite of passage. But for those who have been there, eaten that, go instead to **Jay's Jayburgers** in Silverlake. The peppery slabs are freshly fried, served with a huge tomato slice, and come with a fried egg (aka the Eggburger), just in case you haven't jacked up your cholesterol enough. Chili is free, but it sogs up the bun. Go for the jalapeños instead. No Coke. Pepsi. Also not to be missed while in L.A. is **Fatburger**, which like Tommy's serves chili burgers but with much better chili. Don't miss the chili fries here. Bring Tums. Branches exist all over town, but only one, in West Hollywood, shows *manga* videos. And even Beverly Hills has a junk-food stand open late, but here, of course, it's a *café,* namely the ~~Beverly Hills Café~~. It's a hit with kids on their way home from an after-hours cruise in dad's Lexus or with addled folk just released from the confines of the rock palace Troubadour. It's your basic burgers and fries, but the enclosed patio is a nice addition.

Japanese... Listen to me. There is no other late-night food that will slip more gracefully through your ravaged intestinal tract than ramen, *gyoza* pot stickers, even deep-fried *tonkatsu.* The white rice drapes everything in comforting silence. **Koraku** is absent of ambience, sort of a typical Japanese lunchtime diner circa 1953. It won't win any restaurant awards, but the food is reliable, consistent, and reasonably priced. The perfect west-side place to visit after a karaoke binge is **Mamenoki**, when it's late and cold and all that will do is a nice hot bowl of *oden,* a fish-cake soup. Appropriately, a complimentary bowl of *mame* (cold boiled soybeans) is brought to the table with the menus. They have a full sushi bar and the standard smorgasbord of dishes that old Japanese restaurants catering to Americans feel they have to offer you. But the price is right, the hours are fine, and, in case you just can't stop crooning, there's even a karaoke bar next door (although hours vary). The interior is like an up-country Japanese inn, huge beams and support posts that are supposed to import a rustic feel but actually just remind you of a late-night restaurant on the outskirts of Tokyo catering to salarymen too drunk to make it home from the train station. Fairly new in this location, **Kagetsu-An** serves up what you might call Japanese soul food—*soba* and *udon* noodles in a variety of soups and sauces. They offer more than 30 different noodle dishes, some using homemade pastas, and there's no item over $10. If you're dining alone, there's a huge library of the latest *manga* (Japanese comic books) by the front door.

Thai me up, Thai me down... When you need a dose of genuine Thai food at 3am, there's only one choice:

Sanamluang Cafe. The bright lights may be a shock, and Sammy's (as non-Thai speakers call it) is always crowded, frenetic, and reeking of pungent fish sauce. Especially popular with underground musicians and Thai club kids, it's a cross-section of L.A. nightlife, nearly as varied as the menu. If you want it spicy, get the mint noodles. The Thai iced coffee is the perfect drink before you hit the freeway. Another choice, up in a funky section of Hollywood just around the corner from the Capitol Building, is **Chao Praya**, a Thai landmark for years, long before there was a larb outlet on every corner. It's been a popular musicians' hangout for decades, being convenient to the sound studios in the nabe. Try the roasted chicken and the *mee krob*, a crunchy, sweet noodle dish.

Mexican/Central American... The faded posters on the walls of Old Town Pasadena's **El Toreo Cafe** say it all—this place has been here a while and seen some changes. The menu offers many inventive, unusual seafood dishes—try the abalone soup, if they have any left. Get here early; they close around 11. For a 3am taco or burrito with extra *carnitas*, the best choices are basic stands, like **Benito's Original Taco Shop** on Third in West Hollywood. The bright lights should wake you up, and if they don't the salsa will. The hefty burritos are a must-try, and for to-die-for *pupusas*, Benito's has the stand-market cornered. The **San Salvadore Restaurant** does stay open latish—around midnight—and is a popular hang for dates. For less than $2 you can get a great bean *pupusa*, greasy but without the heavy feeling of a burger. They have the best merengue jukebox anywhere at this hour. Another El Salvadoran treat is **El Cafétal** for *pupusas*, fried yucca, plantains, empanadas, and even *hamburguesas con queso*. Prices are way cheap.

Pizza... I know there must be other places selling pizza in the wee hours, but a friend in the Fairfax district turned me on to **Damiano's Mr. Pizza** years ago, and I just keep coming back. The pizzas aren't quite like John's in New York, but they're far better than anything you'll find at Shakey's. Weird mixtures of toppings (egg and avocado, anybody?), a near-perfect thin crust (although Sicilian-style is also available), and lighting so dim that you won't notice the cheese on your shirt until you get home make it a far more enjoyable dining experience than Canter's, just across the street.

Trendy (the food's not important)... Not too much to say about **Red**, except that it's very, *very* red. Saturated in red. So red that you don't think you'll ever see blue or green or yellow again. And when you go into the cozy adjacent bar, Red Eye, it's red to the nth degree. It's almost hallucinogenic. The clown paintings on the walls are actually a relief after this primary overload. The food is American bistro (meat loaf, grilled *ahi*, summery tomato sauces with pasta, and the usual suspects), the only standout being the chicken for two, a whole bird roasted in apple cider and thyme. Co-owner David Reiss used to manage the Olive, so he knows what works for his industry crowd—a long wait, surly waiters, and mediocre food. The place seats 100 and only accepts reservations (which would be advised) for parties of four or more. There's also **Swingers** in Beverly Hills—a diner for people who wouldn't be caught dead at a kitsch faux-fifties burgerama like Johnny Rockets. They serve up burgers, omelettes, and good breakfasts of every stripe.

Sweets... A good late-night milk shake is harder to find than you'd think. The all-night coffee shops have them but they're never as thick and seriously rich as the artery-clogging concoctions you hanker for. That means a stop at **Double Rainbow** on Melrose for premium ice cream, fresh cookies, and muffins. There's always a crowd of people hanging out front or lounging by the window, emitting almost a coffeehouse vibe, but with sugar instead of caffeine as the rush of choice. For slightly soggier pastries, go to **House of Pies** in Los Feliz, where they also serve breakfast, burgers, and *(quelle surprise!)* pie. If it's late and you're on the east side, they'll do. A true pie lover, however, will hop on the freeway and head for **The Apple Pan** in Rancho Park (north of Culver City), where there's often a wait late at night—with good reason. Their pies are nearly perfect. And, yeah, it's a chain thang, but sometimes you really want to have a gooey **Mrs. Fields** chocolate chip cookie. The WeHo outlet has everything you need to set your teeth hurting. For a far more healthy treat, go across Santa Monica Boulevard and check out **Mani's Bakery,** where you can get decent espresso, flowery teas, and health-conscious pastries. You don't have to go this route of course, but for those on a diet, Mani's has low-fat, sugar-free, organic-wheat pastries that taste much better than they should.

The Index

$$$	$30 or more
$$	$10–$20
$	hard to spend more than $10

The Apple Pan. Fairly basic diner food, but come here for the pies, especially the apple pie with a big dollop of vanilla ice cream. Absolute heaven.... *Tel 310/475–3585. 10801 W. Pico Blvd., Rancho Park. Open till midnight on weekends, 11 the rest of the week. No credit cards.* $$

La Bamba. A wonderful trip around the Caribbean, without leaving your seat in Pasadena. There's very danceable live salsa and steel-drum music, but come for the food. The flan is the best ever, the fried plantains heavenly instead of heavy, and the jerked chicken wonderfully sweet and spicy at the same time. If you're not sure, get the appetizer platter. Rice and black beans come with everything.... *Tel 818/581–9771. 61 N. Raymond Ave., Old Town, Pasadena. Food service stops at 11:30pm on weekends; bar closes at 1am.* $$–$$$

Ben Frank's. In the heart of the Strip, this is where all of Hollywood's nightcrawlers eventually end up, makeup smeared, ectoplasm reeking of smoke. Order meat loaf, a shake, and try to stop the shaking in your hands.... *Tel 310/652–8808. 8585 Sunset Blvd., West Hollywood. Open 24 hours. DC not accepted.* $$

Benita's Fries. The best fries in the world. Nothing else. A basic human right.... *Tel 310/458–2889. 1437 3rd St. Promenade, Santa Monica. Open till midnight on the weekends. No credit cards.* $

Benito's Original Taco Shop. A typical outdoor stand that gives this characterless section of Third Street a reason to exist after midnight. Great burritos. So-so tacos.... *Tel 213/ 938–7427. 8001 W. 3rd St., West Hollywood. Open 24 hours. No credit cards. $*

Beverly Hills Cafe. Popular with kids, basic hamburger-stand quasi-fast food.... *Tel 310/652–1529. 14 N. La Cienega Blvd., Beverly Hills. Open 24 hours. $–$$*

Brooklyn Bagel Bakery. Yes, there are bagels in California. And good ones, too.... *Tel 213/413–4114. 2217 W. Beverly Blvd., Los Angeles. $*

El Cafétal. El Salvadoran fast food: *pupusas,* yucca, hamburgers, and zip in the way of atmosphere, but open until 2am on the weekends. So don't complain.... *Tel 213/669– 9710. 4929 Santa Monica Blvd., East Hollywood. Cash only. $–$$*

Canter's. For 60 years they've been giving heartburn to the good folk of L.A. Critical as a cranky grandmother, reliable as the sunrise. The pastrami is a little dry, the corned beef less so. The pickles are wonderful. And you'd better clean your plate or you'll hear about it later.... *Tel 213/651– 2030. 419 Fairfax Ave., Fairfax. Open 24 hours. AE, D, DC not accepted. $$*

Chao Praya. Thai food that is a wee bit greasy at times. But you can't get a better roasted chicken—you may even be tempted to eat the bones. The dipping sauce is key. Popular with musicians.... *Tel 213/466–6704. 6307 Yucca Ave., Hollywood. Open till 1:30am on weekends. D not accepted. $$*

Ciao Yie. One of the great cross-cultural cuisine experiences in L.A., a blend of Northern Italian and Chinese. Some dishes play it straight, others (like the Chinese barbecued pork linguini) mix it up. Subtle and light in delivery and preparation, this is perfect late-night food.... *Tel 818/578–7501. 54 W. Colorado Blvd., Old Town, Pasadena. Open till midnight (or a little later) on the weekends. $$*

Damiano's Mr. Pizza. A room as dark as the club that just sprung you, fabulous pies of every possible combination, better thin crust than thick, and people who think just like you: sometimes only a pizza will do.... *Tel 213/658–7611. 412 N. Fairfax Ave., Fairfax. Open till 6am. $$*

Denny's. Don't think you're going to see guitars hanging on the walls at this chain outlet. It's typical Denny's food. Lousy. But for some reason musicians and club kids with deadened taste buds stumble in.... *Tel 213/876–6660. 7373 Sunset Blvd., Hollywood. Open 24 hours. $$*

Double Rainbow. Coffees, teas, good cookies and muffins, plus the best chocolate shakes around. Award-winning ice cream.... *Tel 213/655–1986. 7376 Melrose Ave., Los Angeles. Open till midnight. No credit cards. $–$$*

Fatburger. No, this isn't a misprint. The West Hollywood outlet of this greasy grill hosts large-TV screenings of Japanese *manga* videos twice a week, Tuesdays and Fridays. They're animated, violent, high-tech, and go great with fries.... *Tel 213/436–0862. 7450 Santa Monica Blvd., West Hollywood.*

El Floridita. No need to invade. We've got Havana on our doorsteps. This is the place for Cuban expats to congregate, dance the tango, and complain about politics back home. Reliable (but not outstanding) Cuban cuisine, come for the scene—especially on the dance floor. On weekends it's way busy and you probably won't be able to park in the tiny little strip-mall lot.... *Tel 213/871–8612. 1253 N. Vine St., Hollywood. Closes at 1am, the kitchen an hour earlier. $$.*

fusion at pdc. Located in the Blue Whale (aka the Pacific Design Center), this uncrowded newcomer serves great California cuisine at absurdly low prices. The back-to-basics presentation of tasty salads, soups, and fish is an artful contrast to the high-tech decor.... *Tel 310/659–6012. 8687 Melrose Ave., at the Pacific Design Center (enter at San Vicente), West Hollywood. Full dinners till 11pm; limited cocktail menu till 1:30 on weekends. $$–$$$*

Gaucho Grill. Argentine-style cuts of meat, grilled to savory tenderness, smothered in garlic, washed down with a Cristal (Peru) or Pacena (Bolivia) beer or Argentine chardonnay. The atmosphere is way casual, solo-diner friendly.... *Tel 310/394–4966. 1251 Third Street Promenade, Santa Monica.*

Open till midnight on weekends, 11 the rest of the week. D not accepted. $$

Hamburger Haven. One of the *best* late-night burgers around. Covered outdoor patio dining that is very un-WeHo.... *Tel 310/659–8774. 8954 Santa Monica Blvd., West Hollywood. Open till 2am on weekends, 1am the rest of the week. No credit cards.* $

House Of Pies. Pies, natch, as well as standard grill food. Not the best, but not the worst either.... *Tel 213/666–9961. 1869 N. Vermont Ave., Los Feliz. Open till 2am on the weekends, 1am the rest of the week. AE, D, DC not accepted.* $$

Jay's Jayburgers. Real burgers, in a real L.A. burger stand, and stumble-close to The Garage (see The Club Scene). A most reliable stop.... *Tel 213/666–5204. 4481 Santa Monica Blvd. (at Virgil), Silver Lake. Open till 4am on weekends, 1am the rest of the week. No credit cards.* $

Kagetsu-An. The clientele at this noodle-rama is mostly Japanese, always a good sign. It's cheap, offers a full range of *soba* and *udon* dishes, and you'll never feel guilty for eating here late at night.... *Tel 213/613–1479. 318 E. 2nd St. #A, Little Tokyo. Open till 3am Mon–Sat. AE, D, DC not accepted.* $–$$

Koraku. Chinese food done in a Japanese style, Japanese food done in a greasy-spoon style. But the most expensive thing on the 70-dish menu is the eel rice bowl at $8.25. Eat here.... *Tel 213/687–4972. 314 E. 2nd St., Little Tokyo. Open till 3am Mon–Sat, till midnight on Sun. No credit cards.* $–$$

Little Ricky's. Heart-friendly gourmet Cuban-Mexican food, convivial staff, and a feeling that the artists whose art is on the walls come by here to eat. For my money, this is the hippest and most interesting eatery in Pasadena. Their hours vary greatly; sometimes they stay open till 1:30am. It all depends on what's happening, so call.... *Tel 818/440–0306. 39 S. Fair Oaks Ave., Old Town, Pasadena.* $–$$

Mamenoki. A west-side Japanese eatery that's open way late and has better food than you deserve at this hour. Plus a selection of eight sakes.... *Tel 310/444–1432. 2068 Sawtelle Blvd., Los Angeles. Open till 2am Tue–Sat, midnight on Sun. AE, D, DC not accepted. $$*

Mani's Bakery. Part bakery, part coffeehouse, part gift store. This is a gourmet bakery that also features low-fat, sugar-free treats using organically grown wheat and real chocolate.... *Tel 310/659–5955. 8801 Santa Monica Blvd., West Hollywood. Open till 3am on weekends, 1am the rest of the week. DC not accepted. $–$$*

Mrs. Field's Cookies. Cookies. Need we say more?... *Tel 310/659–9330. 8910 Santa Monica Blvd., West Hollywood.*

Norm's. A classic coffee shop where what you see is what you get. Cheap, fast, basic Americana, pre-nouvelle cuisine.... *Tel 310/450–6889. 1601 Lincoln Blvd., Santa Monica. Open 24 hours. AE, D, DC not accepted. $*

Operetta. This European-style bakery and deli has better-than-average pastries and standard salads and gourmet meats. Eat 'em here or get 'em to go.... *Tel 213/852–7000. 8223 3rd St., Los Angeles. Open 24 hours. $$.*

Pinot Hollywood. A major Hollywood hang, with California-bistro food that gets regular raves from local foodies. Smoked salmon rolled around a sour-sweet cream mousse, quail stuffed with wild mushrooms and pecans. Are you salivating yet?... *Tel 213/461–8800. 1448 N. Gower St., Hollywood. Open till midnight during the week, till 1am weekends. $$$*

Pentola Taverna. Elegant yet approachable, quiet and mature. This is the antithesis of the frenzy on the Third Street Promenade, just a few feet away. Excellent California cuisine.... *Tel 310/451–1963. 312 Wilshire Blvd., Santa Monica. Dinner until 11:30pm on weekends, 10:30pm the rest of the week. D, DC not acepted. $$$*

Red. Just walking into Red is a taste treat—if you're a believer of color therapy. Otherwise, carb up before you come in. The very so-so bistro-style menu is small but adequate, the beers many, the wine list selective. There's seating outside on the sidewalk, the perch of choice is in one of the high-backed booths facing the clown pictures in the adjacent room and bar area. Unless you're an obvious big spender or a celeb, the service can be slow.... *Tel 213/937–0331. 7450 Beverly Blvd., Los Angeles. Kitchen open till 11pm Sun–Thur, midnight the rest of the week. $$$*

Reel Inn. This is the sister outlet of one of Malibu's best (and most affordable) fresh-fish restaurants. The decor is basic—long picnic tables, a haphazard mix of marine accessories hanging on the walls. It's counter service only, but at $10 for a yellowtail dinner, who's complaining?... *Tel 310/395–5538. 1220 Third Street Promenade, Santa Monica. Kitchen open till 10:30 or 11pm on weekends, depending on the crowd. AE, D, DC not accepted. $$.*

Sanamluang Cafe. The absolute best after-3am food choice when you want greasy, hot, fried, and savory Asian dishes. Or vegetarian, steamed, garlicky, and spicy. Or all of the above. They cover the Thai-Chinese menu much better than you deserve this late at night. Expect it to be crowded all the way until 4 when it closes.... *Tel 213/660–8006. 5176 Hollywood Blvd., Hollywood. $$*

San Salvadore Restaurant. Two *pupusas* and a *liquado* will set you back less than $6 at this comfy El Salvadoran hang-out in a strip mall across from Los Angeles City College. A fab jukebox and maybe live music earlier in the night.... *Tel 213/913–7972. 712 N. Vermont Ave. (at Melrose), East Hollywood. No credit cards. $*

Ships. The most evocative Jetsons-era coffee shop in the city and a major nostalgic twinge for homegrown Angelenos. Everyone has been here after their prom.... *Tel 310/839–2347. 10705 Washington Blvd. (at Overland), Culver City. AE, DC not accepted. Open 24 hours. $*

Swingers. Omelettes, burgers, fifties diner food with a nineties delivery and price. Reliable but not fab. Popular with too-cool scene makers.... *Tel 213/653–5858. 820 Beverly Blvd., Los Angeles. Open till 2am during the week, 4am on weekends. $$$*

Tommy's. This is the real thing, home of the messiest burgers in the city. A natural cure for a hangover. At 3am you'll be waiting in line with a true cross-section of L.A. late-night lifers.... *Tel 213/389–9060. 2575 Beverly Blvd., Los Angeles. Open 24 hours. No credit cards. $*

El Toreo Cafe. This little hole-in-the-wall feels like some place off the *zocolo* (central square) in Mexico City. Twin faded posters of presidents face each other on the walls: one of John F. Kennedy circa 1962 and the other of the presidents of Mexico, circa Lopez Portillo. The menu is fairly typical, but also includes some outstanding rarities like abalone or octopus soup.... *Tel 818/793–2577. 21 S. Fair Oaks Ave., Old Town, Pasadena. Open until 11. AE, D, DC not accepted. $$*

Van Go's Ear. A wonderful if slightly funky all-night restaurant in an old wooden house in Venice, they have everything from eggs and rolls to sandwiches and protein drinks. Excellent food at a great price.... *Tel 310/314–0022. 796 Main St., Venice. No credit cards. $$*

Yangtze. The decor sucks, the menu is too broad to be on target, but if you're in Santa Monica and are hungry for something vaguely Asian (Chinese or Thai or Japanese) and just can't decide, this is your only choice. At least the sushi is cheap. Everything else is better than a cafeteria—barely.... *Tel 310/260–1994. 1333 Third Street Promenade, Santa Monica. Open till midnight on weekends, 11pm the rest of the week. D not accepted. $–$$*

Ye Olde King's Head. Hard-core British pub food, come here for the fish 'n' chips, the bangers, and the beer.... *Tel 310/451–1402. 116 Santa Monica Blvd., Santa Monica. Kitchen closes around 11pm on the weekends. D, DC not accepted. $$*

down
and
dirty

All-night pharmacies... For locations of **Sav-on 24-hour pharmacies**, call 800/627–2866.

American Express... Amex offices are located at 327 N. Beverly Dr. in Beverly Hills and at 901 W. 7th St. downtown, as well as throughout the city. If you lose your card, or if it's stolen, call 800/528–4800; to report lost or stolen traveler's checks, call 800/221–7282.

Babysitters... First ask the concierge if your hotel offers child care services (most larger hotels do). Otherwise, call the **Baby-Sitters Guild** (tel 818/552–2229; P.O. Box 4319, Glendale, CA 91222-0319), a 24-hour on-call service which has been providing mature, bonded sitters since 1948.

Buses... Los Angeles has two major bus systems. Santa Monica's blue buses cover the west side, from Pacific Palisades to Venice on the coast and inland along major streets like Wilshire, Santa Monica, and Pico Boulevards. It's best for shorter trips between Santa Monica, Brentwood, and the UCLA campus. The much farther-ranging yellow county buses are more expensive, but will get you between Hollywood, downtown, and points south. The Santa Monica Municipal Bus Lines cost $.50 for basic fare, $1.25 for the 10 bus (which goes to Downtown L.A.), and operates between 6am and midnight (depending on the line). Call 310/451–5444 for point-to-point information. The Los Angeles County Metropolitan Transit Authority buses cost $1.35 and up, depending on freeway or express service and distance traveled; 35¢ for transfers. Call 213/626–4455 for bus schedule and point-to-point information, 6am to 8:30pm during the week, 8am to 6pm on weekends. Some buses do run all night, but it varies with the line.

Car rental... For rental cars, all the major companies are available. I usually go with **Dollar** (tel 800/800–4000) or **Enterprise** (tel 213/467–2277) because they're close by, but **Alamo** (tel 800/327–9633), **Avis** (tel 800/331–1212), **Budget** (tel 800/527–0700), **General** (tel 800/327–7607), **Hertz** (tel 800/654–3131), **National** (tel 800/328–4567), and **Thrifty** (tel 800/367–2277) also have locations throughout the area.

Driving around... Of course you can get from point A to point B using the freeways, but often that's not a wise choice—as any Angeleno knows all too well. There is no such thing as rush hour here. These days, a bumper-to-bumper traffic jam is liable to materialize on any stretch of freeway at any given moment, whether it's 7 in the morning or high noon. The only time safe from clog-ups are late at night, and then you have much more dangerous problems, like inebriates driving at high speeds. For getting between **Downtown** and **Santa Monica**, consider the major city streets: **Venice**, **Olympic**, **Pico**, **Wilshire**, or **Santa Monica**. The lights may slow you down, but there will be fewer obvious drunks or scary accidents. Going west into **Hollywood**, avoid Sunset and Hollywood boulevards when possible (especially on weekends), taking instead **Fountain** or **Franklin**. Streets running south out of Hollywood are usually pretty clear. The fastest way to get to **Santa Monica** from **Hollywood** is probably taking **La Brea** south to the **Santa Monica Freeway**, avoiding the crush around Downtown.

Since there are now so many No Left Turn signs on **Melrose**, it flows better than it used to, but it can still be a nightmare with people trying to park. Running parallel a few blocks to the south, **Beverly Boulevard** is a much smoother alternative. The freeways switch names in different areas, but it's not that hard to keep track of them. The **101** Freeway is called the Hollywood north of Downtown, and just beyond Studio City it changes its name to the Ventura Freeway.

A major north-south throughway that connects outlaying desert-edge communities, such as Pomona, to the **Interstate 5** (which feeds into the Hollywood) is called the Santa Ana Freeway south of Downtown. North of Downtown the 5 becomes the Golden State Freeway. The **2** is called the Harbor Freeway south of Downtown, and the Pasadena Freeway north of Downtown. Running east-west and draining out onto the Pacific Coast Highway (or Route 1), Interstate 10 is called the San Bernardino Freeway east of Downtown, and the Santa Monica Freeway west of Downtown. The **405** is always the San Diego Freeway. Avoid it if you can.

For regular traffic conditions on the freeways, tune your radio to **KNX 1070 AM**. They have updates every six minutes.

When parking anywhere in **West Hollywood** or **West L.A.**, look for limitations on the parking signs. Around **Melrose**, **Westwood**, **Santa Monica**, and the **Sunset Strip** in particular, the parking laws are very restrictive and enforced around the clock. Some meters require feeding until 8pm, while *Resident Only* parking keeps you off of the side streets. If you block people's driveways you'll probably get towed. Use parking lots in either Westwood or Santa Monica.

You can turn right on a red light after coming to a full stop unless it's posted otherwise. For many Angelenos, a yellow light means speed up, so don't jump out when the light turns green for you.

By all means, the most important thing to carry with you, no matter how long you've lived here, is the latest **Thomas Guide** map book. This is more important than remembering your wallet, your make-up, or your shoes. And if you don't have one, most bookstores and newsstands carry the line.

A note on general road safety: The random freeway shootings, shootings at people who blinked their high-beams, and bump 'n' rob accidents seem to be off the front pages now. Still, if you get into a fender-bender with someone, pull off into a well-lighted area. If they are typical, honest citizens with no mayhem in mind, they'll probably just speed off anyway.

If you get pulled over by the LAPD or Highway Patrol, stay in your car. Roll down the window and offer your license. Be polite and do NOT get out of your car unless told to do so. During the weekends, police set up roadblocks on popular cruising streets (Hollywood Boulevard, especially), turning back cars and doing random sobriety checks.

Emergencies... Like in most U.S. cities, **call 911** for police, fire, highway patrol, or in the case of a life-threatening medical emergency. Other numbers: **AAA—Auto Club of Southern California**, 800/400–4222 or 310/747–6800. **USC Medical Center Emergency Rooms**, 213/226–6706. **Legal Aid**, 213/487-3320.

Festivals and special events...

January: In Chinatown, **Chinese New Year** (tel 213/617–0396; N. Broadway at Sunset Blvd.) is celebrated with a dragon parade, great food, and a fireworks bonanza.

February: The **Pan African Film Festival** (tel 213/296-7233) is *the* film event of the year for some of the best international films that you'll never see at your local cineplex. Usually held in the first two weeks of February at various theaters around town. L.A. gives **Mardi Gras** a nod Downtown at the site of the city's original pueblo. Expect tacos, piñatas, drunks, and fireworks. The **Los Angeles Bach Festival** (tel 213/385–1341; First Congregational

Church, 540 S. Commonwealth Ave., Los Angeles) happens over ten days in late February and early March.

March: **The Los Angeles Contemporary Exhibition** (tel 213/957–1777; LACE, 6522 Hollywood Blvd., Hollywood), the influential gallery and exhibition space hosts a series of new music concerts.

April: The **Thai New Year Songkran Festival** (tel 818/780–4200; 8225 Coldwater Canyon, North Hollywood) is more family-oriented than the Chinese New Year's celebration, starting during the day and winding up after dark. It includes a Miss Songkran beauty contest, children's performances, and the best fast food you'll ever eat.

May: **Cinco de Mayo** doesn't always happen on May 5th, the date of Mexican Independence, but no matter. It's celebrated Downtown on Broadway, between 1st and 7th, with a day-long (and into the evening) party. **UCLA Pow Wow** (tel 310/206–7513; Intramural Field, UCLA Campus, Westwood), a two-day event, brings together members of various Native American tribes to share their culture. Continues until 11pm. The three-day **Annual Dance Roots Festival** (tel 213/485–2437; Los Angeles Theatre Center, 514 S. Spring St., Downtown) focuses on all aspects of dance: social, traditional, classical, concert. The **Annual UCLA Jazz and Reggae Festival**, traditionally held on Memorial Day weekend, is an all-day and into-the-evening free concert series (with a huge food and crafts marketplace). The Melnitz Theater on the UCLA campus hosts the **Asian Pacific Film & Video Festival** (tel 213/680–3004), a premier source for Asian Pacific culture on video and film, especially from artists working in the U.S.

June: **California Plaza Moonlight and Matinees**; free concerts, with everything from jazz to Okinawan folk-pop. Check the *L.A. Weekly* or the *Downtown News* for listings. Runs through September (tel 213/687–2159; 300–350 S. Grand Ave., Downtown). The evening shows start at 8pm on Fridays and Saturdays in the Watercourt, or in the Spiral Court at the plaza. **African Fete** (tel 213/687–2159; California Plaza, 350 S. Grand Ave., Downtown), an annual free concert series held in early June, features some of the best-known African musicians, both traditional and pop-oriented. **Summer Nights at the Ford** (tel 213/466–1767; John Anson Ford Amphitheatre, 2580 Cahuenga Blvd., Hollywood); classical, jazz, opera, pop, world music—you want it, it's here in this cozy (1,200 seat) outdoor venue. The series starts in mid-June and runs until Labor Day. At the **Playboy Jazz Festival** (tel 310/659–4080; at the Hollywood Bowl, 2301 N. Highland Ave., Hollywood) you'll see why America's great music form is the kind that works best in the Hollywood Bowl. The festival only lasts a few days in mid-June, but the music is continuous and world-class, running from Dixieland to fusion to blues to Salsa. Also at the Bowl, the two-night annual **Mariachi USA Festival** (tel 800/627–4224; at the Hollywood Bowl, 2301 N. Highland Ave., Hollywood) always sells out, and with good reason. Great fireworks, the Ballet Folklorico, and music that will make you cry. Tons o' fun. The **Annual Festival of Preservation** (tel 310/206–3456; Melnitz Theatre, UCLA Campus, Westwood) shows celluloid gems from the vast archives at UCLA and other international sources, ranging from early silents to recent masterpieces and feature films to newsreels. The **Los Angeles Gay & Lesbian Pride Celebration** (tel 213/656–6553; West Hollywood Park at San Vicente Blvd., and nearby locations, West Hollywood) weekend climaxes (so to speak) with a party on Sunday that runs way late. It's always *too* crowded, but good parties always are.

July: **Fourth of July fireworks** shows blast off at Dodger Stadium (tel 213/224–1400; 1000 Elysian Park Ave., Elysian Park) and the Hollywood Bowl (tel 213/972–7300; 2301 Highland Ave., Hollywood). **Annual Lotus Festival** (tel 213/485–1310; Echo Park Lake, Park and Glendale Aves., Los Angeles), a weekend event that runs into the evening, bringing together Asian and Pacific cultures from all over the city for food, art, and wandering bands. Plus, the lotuses are flowering in the lake, always an exhilarating sight. The **Bon Odori Festival** (tel 213/680–9130; L.A. Hongwanji Betsuin Temple, 815 E. First St., Little Tokyo), is the best mid-July street party around. *Obon* is celebrated throughout the city for the next two months, but I like this one because it's in Little Tokyo, the cultural heart for ex-pat Japanese. Starts at 5pm. The **Santa Monica Pier** free concert series (tel 310/458–8900; at the corner of Ocean Ave. and Colorado, Santa Monica) has ten shows every summer through August, from Latin salsa to reggae and jazz. Concerts usually start about 7:30pm. The **L.A. Shake-**

speare Festival's (tel 213/489–1121; various locations around the city) stagings are held in the evening, about 30 performances per season. Usually free, or maybe a donation of food for the needy; runs into August. At the **Hollywood Bowl Summer Festival** (tel 213/972–7300; 2301 N. Highland Ave., Hollywood), it's time to pack a light dinner, champagne, and your cell phone. Includes performances by the L.A. Philharmonic, the Hollywood Bowl Orchestra, top jazz performers, and international artists. Runs through September.

August: The **Annual Sunset Junction Street Faire** (tel 213/661–7777; 3,600-4,000 blocks of Sunset Blvd., Silver Lake), held in late August, is an excuse for the Silver Lake, Echo Park, and Los Feliz communities to assert their very unique east sider-ness. Gay, straight, Asian, Latino-it's a nonstop party for two days.

September: The Chinese have been celebrating the **Annual Chinese Moon Festival** (tel 213/617–0396; various locations around Chinatown, Downtown) for two thousand years. They've got it down. Music, dancers, martial arts displays, and (if it's not too smoggy) a view of the moon.

October: The **American Film Institute's Los Angeles International Film Festival** (tel 213/856–7707; various theaters around the city) has more than 200 screenings of the rare, unusual, new, and foreign. Best deal is getting a full festival pass for $200.

November: **Dia de los Muertos** (tel 213/881–6444; Galeria Otra Vez, Self Help Graphics, 3802 Ceasar Chavez Blvd., East Los Angeles); East L.A.'s Day of the Dead celebration, a must for anyone who wants to understand what L.A. is really all about. Families, music, art, great food.

December: Even though it's hard to get into the spirit of the season in L.A.'s unchanging climate, the **Los Posadas** (tel 213/687–4344; Olvera St., Downtown) candlelight Christmas procession works nicely anyway. It marks the journey of Joseph and Mary to Bethlehem. The processions go on every evening for nine days. The best part comes when the kids get turned loose on the candy-filled piñatas. Don't even think of driving in Hollywood on the night of the **Hollywood Christmas Parade** (tel 213/469–2337; Hollywood Blvd., Hollywood). Masses of people throng the streets, celebrities pass by in floats, marching bands thunder. Stay home and watch it on TV.

Newspapers, fanzines, weeklies... As you cruise the bars, clubs, coffeehouses, bookstores, and restaurants of the night, you'll inevitably trip over a pile of homemade fanzines, the throwaway culture's equivalent of folk art. Usually subsisting on ads, and the mania of one driven individual with a Mac and a low-overhead lifestyle, they can be a window on the culture of a city most daytime-dwellers never get a glimpse of. The listings may not always be accurate or up-to-date, but the editorial, despite the inevitable typo here and there, will be appropriately opinionated and cliquish. These people *know* what's going on—or at least they think they do. More important, they care. Here are a few on the current roster worth looking at. ***Boing Boing:*** Computer weirdness. ***Dragzine:*** Drag-queen mania. ***Giant Robot:*** Pop culture with a Pacific Rim take. ***Lounge:*** Lounge culture.

Among the larger circulation, weekly, free papers, look for the following. ***L.A. Reader:*** The print is too small for dim lights, but the listings are accurate and the reviewers intelligent. ***L.A. Weekly:*** This offspring of the old ***L.A. Free Press*** is the fattest of the weeklies and suffers from severe eye clutter. But everybody advertises in it, and their extensive listing guides, ranging from films to the Internet, is a marvel. Their music reviews are far better and hipper than the *L.A. Times* (which isn't saying much). Best dance listings in town. ***Los Angeles View:*** A fairly recent upstart, the ***View*** is growing well and has a staff of literate, humorous, opinionated writers. Their listings are good, especially for the West Side. For gay publications, ***4-Front:*** Fairly new, but with good, accurate listings and funny adult video reviews. Good coverage of what's happening in WeHo (West Hollywood) gay/dance clubs. ***Female FYI:*** Also fairly new; focuses on dyke culture. ***Frontiers:*** The most consistently readable and newsworthy.

When it comes to major newspapers, there's only one: ***The Los Angeles Times.*** Despite its phlegmatic reputation, it's the only paper in the country that stacks up to the *New York Times.* I won't get into kvetching about the paper since I've free-lanced for them fairly often in the last 15 years, but I will recommend looking out for a few bylines: Heidi Seigmund Cuda covers clubs and nightlife in the daily "Calendar" section; Kristine McKenna writes about film and art for the daily and Sunday "Calendar";

LOS ANGELES ◟ DOWN AND DIRTY

Jonathon Gold writes about the city's burgeoning ethnic restaurant scene in Thursday's "Food" section; and Michelle Huneven handles other restaurant reviews in Friday's "Calendar."

Surprisingly, L.A. has only two city magazines, **Buzz** and the suddenly readable ***Los Angeles Magazine***. They both have decent listings though heavily weighted toward upscale nightlife. *Buzz* has its ear closer to the ground when it comes to street-level events.

Online information... There are more than 3,500 World Wide Web sites that relate to L.A., 89 local Internet providers, and 18 coffeehouses with connections to the Net. There are also hundreds of bulletin board systems for less graphical cruising. Look in the weekly *Recycler* for the most complete listings. For a general introduction, go to @LA, which you'll find at http://emporium.turnpike.net/A/atLA/index.html. Other sources include: **Beyond Baroque Bookstore** (http://www.crl.com/~jamison), *BUZZ* **Magazine** (http://www.buzzmag.com/buzz/), **Club Fais Do-Do** (http://www.spinach.com:80/isis/), **Club Link—club listings** (http://www.clublink.com), **Concert listings** (http://calendar.com/cgi-bin/music-search?state=CA), **Dutton's Bookstore**—includes bookstore events (http://www.earthlink.net/~duttons/), **Earthquake activity over past three days** (http://seec.gps.caltech.edu/), **Free Net Home Page (source for other Web sites)** (http://lafn.org:80/welcome.html), **Frontiers Newsmagazine** (http://www.frontiersweb.com), **House of Blues** (http://www.hob.com/), **Industry Java and Jive** (http://www.primenet.com/~industry), **Interact! CD-ROM Store** (http://www.interactcd.com), *Irish News*—**newspaper for ex-pat Irish** (http://www.gyw.com/laweb/inews), **Jazz & Blues clubs in L.A.** (http://www.dnai.com/~lmcohen/lacd.html), **L.A. (The Bookstore)** see L.A. Online, **L.A. Dodgers baseball** (http://www.ugcs.caltech.edu/~magyer/baseball/dodgers.html), **L.A. Kings Hockey** (http://web1.starwave.com/nhl/clb/los.html), **L.A. Online** (includes *L.A. Reader* text, other local newspapers, movie & club listings, ads—this is a BBS, 14.4 baud, 8-N-1; 213/936–1160; 310/372–4050; 310/445–0633; 818/577–2131), **Laserium shows at Griffith Park** (http://www.laserium.com/schedules/LA_sched.html), **Los Angeles County Museum of Art** (http://www.lacma.org), **Los Angeles Opera** (http://www.primenet.com/~thoward/lamco/), **Los Angeles Public Library**—

includes library events (http://www.carl.org/cinfo.html), **91X (91.1 FM)**—a radio station, this includes profiles of local bands (http://www.cerf.net/91x.html), **Midnight Special Bookstore**—includes bookstore events (http://www.cinenet.net:80/msbooks/homepage.html), **Genghis Cohen Cantina** (http://i-site.com/), **Santa Anita Park** (horse racing; http://www.santaanita.com), **Sex/adult entertainment/strip shows** (http://www.paranoia.com/faq/Los Angeles.txt), **Southern California Web Sites** (http://www.directnet.com/~scb/online.html), **West Hollywood Guide** (ftp://ftp.netcom.com/pub/jc/jclark/web/wehoweb.html), and **World Cafe** (http://www.worldcafe-la.com).

Radio... Ann The Raven: KPCC 89.3 FM, Sat, midnight to 2am. Blues. **Brave New World**: KCRW 89.9 FM, Mon, Wed–Fri, 10pm to midnight. Alt.rock to L.A. Cool. **Citybilly**: KPCC 89.3 FM, Mon, 8–10pm. The best in country-folk roots and experimental. **Dr. Demento**: KSCA 101.9 FM, Sun, 10pm–midnight. The records you never bought, but always wanted. **Folk Masters**: KPCC 89.3 FM, Mon, 11pm–midnight. World roots music. **Go Zone**: KCRW 89.9 FM, Sat & Sun, 9pm–midnight. Indie rock and unsigned weirdness. **Ian Whitcomb Show**: KPCC 89.3 FM, Wed, 10pm–midnight. Idiosyncratic view of popular music from a British legend. **Jazz at the Kennedy Center**: KPCC 89.3 FM, Thurs, 11pm–midnight. Hosted by Billy Taylor; jazz interviews and live jams. **Jazzset**: KPCC 89.3 FM, Tues, 10–11pm. Hosted by Branford Marsalis; jazz from around the world. **Making The Music**: KPCC 89.3 FM, Tues, 11pm–midnight. Hosted by Wynton Marsalis; jazz interviews and music. **Molotov Cocktail Hour**: KXLU 88.9 FM, Tues, 11pm–midnight. Tiki and lounge music from hell. **Psychotechnics**: KXLU 88.9 FM, Wed, midnight–2am. Harsh, unpleasant, keeps you awake. **Red Eye**: KCRW 89.9 FM, Sat, midnight–3am. Ambient, trip-hop, L.A. Cool. **Reggae House Party**: KMAX 107.1 FM, Fri & Sat, 12:30–3am. Soothing Caribbean music, from ska and calypso to soca, dancehall, and roots reggae. **Rhythm & Blues Time Capsule**: KPCC 89.3 FM, Fri, 10pm–1am. Rare oldies, forgotten tracks. **Surf Patrol**: KMAX 107.1 FM, Sat & Sun, 5–7am. Surf music, surf reports, surf gossip. **The Music Never Stops**: KPFK 90.7 FM, Fri, 8–10pm. Grateful Dead Forever! **Worldwide Jazz With Gene Parrish**: KUSC 91.5 FM, Sat, 10–11pm. Global riffs.

LOS ANGELES ⟨ DOWN AND DIRTY

Rail... The same fares and phone number (310/626–4455) that apply to L.A. Metro buses (see "Buses" above) also apply to our skimpy, three-line light rail system. But don't bother considering this as an option. The system is incomplete and restricted. If you need to take a train, know that the **Blue Line** connects downtown L.A. to Long Beach, the **Red Line** runs underground just five stops in the downtown area, and the **Green Line** links Norwalk near Orange County to Los Angeles International Airport.

Taxis... If you're not downtown, it's difficult to hail a cab. Cab stands can be found at airports, major hotels, and at Union Station downtown, but if you don't want to chance it you can order a car in advance through either **Bell Cab** (tel 213/221–2355), **L.A. Taxi** (213/627–7000), or **United Independent Taxi** (tel 213/483–7604). Since L.A. is a sprawling city, and the fares are high ($1.90 at the flagdrop and $1.60 per mile thereafter), most cab rides will be fairly expensive; $10 for a short trip is not unusual. A service charge is added to rides from LAX.

Time... Call 213/853–1212 for the time.

Weather... Call Los Angeles Weather Information (tel 213/554–1212) to get the forecast.